THEOLOGICAL DISCUSSIONS

ON LIFE, CREATION AND THE NATURE OF THE DIVINE

PASTOR RICHARD LAMBERT

THEOLOGICAL DISCUSSIONS

ON LIFE, CREATION AND THE NATURE OF THE DIVINE

PASTOR RICHARD LAMBERT

Kravitz & Sons

INNOVATORS IN PUBLISHING, MARKETING AND ADVERTISING

Kravitz and Sons LLC
204 E Arlington Blvd. Suite B
Greenville, NC 27858

Published by Kravitz and Sons LLC.

ISBN: 979-8-89639-622-2 (sc)
ISBN: 979-8-89639-621-5 (e)

CONTENTS

Documented Discussions with others

This book is dedicated

To the internal man who

are made up of spiritual and

Celestial people of God who are

Full of Innocence, Love and Peace.

AUTHORS PREFACE

I've been a theologian and spiritualist for 24 years. I'd like to give you what I have been learning according to the scriptures about life after death. That there is spiritual knowledge of the spiritual world where heaven and hell are said to exist, also the nature of the Divine Life, and the world of spirits were men come together after they leave the body. How the "spiritual" part of us such as our thoughts and affections coincide with the physical part of us such as our speech and actions. Please join me in our discovery and discussion of both the invisible and visible worlds. My mission is to bring spiritual consciences to all people.

This book contains actual responses to discussions I have had with others. There was a particular group online that I was invited to by a good friend. The discussions were indeed highly intellectual. Many of them were and are sharp as to the Hebrew and Greek understanding of the word of God as well as some of them being Israelites themselves. Some considered themselves as Jews, some as Israelites, and others as black Israelites. They were all practicing devout men in their religious field. Most of them are very involved with the life and teachings of the Torah also known as the Pentateuch which are the first five books of Moses. Some of them hold the Torah more sacred than the Messiah. Others hold the Messiah more sacred than the Torah. The Messiah meaning Christ is also known to them in Hebrew as Yeshua, and God is rather called by them YHWH (Yah-Wey). We will also use OT in short for Old Testament. You may find these names being used quite often in the following discussions.

I have learned a lot from them as well as them from me. The purpose of this book is twofold. The first is to establish that there is a vast difference between natural and spiritual concepts. Many people confuse them as to what they are and mistaken natural concepts (which make up many of their religious views) for spiritual ones, when most of the time they are only in an outward religious idea concerning the Word, the church and salvation and even the Divine itself. The second is to encourage all Christians to be inspired to study and think more spiritually concerning the

Word of God and not so much according to the letter. *"For the letter killeth, but the spirit giveth life."* All can be sure to know that the bible according to its literal sense gives a natural understanding for natural men, but the same bible as to its literal meaning has a spiritual meaning within it and this is for all those who desire to live and think in a spiritual way concerning the Word of God. You can be sure that the whole Word has within it a spiritual sense that can only be revealed unto those of whom it said that the Holy Spirit will *"lead you and guide you into all truth."* What I mean is that the Lord cannot give you a spiritual understanding directly by the Holy Spirit unless you are open to hear and receive from him in the spirit. This is why many of them could not receive his sayings, for what they understood naturally He meant it spiritually. This is also why the Lord told them that his words are *"spirit and are life"*. It is understood that the Lord is the Word and that He was in heaven before He came to earth. Consequently, the Word was heavenly before it became earthly, spiritual before it became natural, and the Lord himself possessed a spiritual body before He put a natural one. Let us strive therefore to know the Lord not just as to the literal sense of the letter, but as to the spiritual sense of it, for this is His spirit and life.

For confidentiality purposes the names of those with whom the discussions are with were changed to maintain the integrity of their privacy. Also I have given titles to every discussion in order to give an idea of what the discussion is about.

I would like to thank The Lord our God and his son Jesus Christ for enabling me to hold conversation with such highly intelligent men who caused me to dig deep in the well and bring forth that which was good for them and me.

INTRODUCTION

For the sake of understanding the points presented in the following discussions, it is necessary to give some detailed explanation of what is meant when the term mind or spirit is used. When we speak of the mind we are talking about the spiritual faculties of which it consists, such as the will, understanding, memory, and rationality. When we speak of the spirit we are talking about the quality of life that one has or is inspired into one from another. Sometimes they are used interchangeably. How they are used depends upon how the subject matter is approached. This introduction will serve as a foundation for other spiritual terms and meanings to be presented in the following discussions. Many do not give an actual account of what the spiritual is. Here is mine.

What is Spiritual- The transcending of physical things are spiritual. Thus all things immaterial or intangible, such as: The will which is comprised of Feelings, Attitudes, Moods, Emotions and the understanding which is comprised of thought, Memory and Rationality.

FEELINGS - Feelings are affections that are inwardly received. Example: I was affected with good feelings when that happened to me. Affections make feelings. Example: How did this affect you or how did this make you feel? Affections are of various kinds and species and are felt in our mind as inner emotions such as sadness, depression, despair or happiness, joy, ecstasy, and this materializes in the body and becomes a smile or a sad face. Thus the body is used by the mind to express itself. The beginning of these actions are in the brain into which life inflows, actuating it so that life may be present in the body of the person. Whereby, you have the mind and body together. The life of the mind is immaterial and thus distinct from the body. Mind and body is when the life of the mind flows into the brain actuating it and making it alive not from (the brain) itself but from the life of the mind that dwells within it. By this means the mind is thereby present within the body by being present within the brain. The brain is an organ of life. It is not life nor does it produce life it receives life. The brain is a physical and material substance accommodated to the reception of life. Thus life goes into it and affects it. Physical or material things cannot produce nonphysical or immaterial things. Life is immaterial and intangible nonphysical. It first becomes materialized or physical in the brains, which is accommodated to the reception of the faculties of the mind. These areas or sections of the brain such as the cerebrum where thinking, learning, remembering and deciding takes place, is where the mind is seated in the brains acting upon it, and from there goes to all the senses of the body according to the arrangements of their order from the brain. This is why thoughts are in the head and not anywhere else in the body. This same section though is what allows the person to see, hear, smell, taste, and touch in the body. The cerebellum section of the brain is how the person controls body movement and balance in the body. The medulla section of the brain is how the person keeps his heart beating, lungs taking in air, and the stomach digesting food. Therefore the first thing formed in the womb is the head and then body. For this is where the

life is seated and from there is sent throughout the body. Once the body dies the mind cannot be seated in the brains, because of the malfunction of the body due to incidents directly or indirectly to the brain. What is therefore left is the mind with its thoughts and affections continued on the outside of the body. This is now a separate entity called a spirit.

ATTITUDES- Ones own perspective outlook on life going forth in a positive or negative expression. They are used to communicate to others the will of our minds. They are also used as our response to things done to us. Attitudes can be inspired into us and affect us in a positive or negative way. Attitudes are used to outwardly express a determined mind. A bad attitude shows that one is overcome by bad things. It is as if they are saying they have a right be feel bad and that they are going to spread it all around. A good attitude shows one is overcome by good things and they too feel they have a right to feel good and to spread it all around. They are also used as a wall or stance to keep out things that impose themselves against one's own belief system. Attitudes can be looked at as "determined emotions". Such as "I am determined to be happy or sad, angry or self controlled. It is a way to project ones emotions.

EMOTIONS- Emotions are inner feelings that are expressed in the body. They are inner feelings build up to the point that the body is used as an exhalation of these feelings in order for them to pass through the body. The mind inhabits these inner emotions, but because it is adjoined to the brain it uses the body to express those inner emotions that are within it. Like an outlet draining out wastes that are continually coming in lest the waste backs up and destroy everything within. It is an outlet for the release of inner pressure to escape. This is how we can continually drain our minds of negative energy. Talk out your problems with someone you love and trust. Even a psychologist for they are there to hear and help you drain your mind of the inner emotions that are in it. Above all you can pray fervently about it for in this way you relieve your spirit of any trouble, because you know he hears you. It is important to speak out what is kept in you so that it doesn't build up and become unmanageable. Recreational activity is another great way to defuse build up emotions. Examples are meditation, recollecting our thoughts, inhaling and exhaling or taking a walk, all in an effort to manage our emotions. Manageable emotions are what can be called controlled. Unmanaged emotions are what are called uncontrolled. They are like eruptions of a volcano which can do great harm.

MOOD(S)-The state of the mind given over to good or bad affection(s) as a whole. People who are sad as a whole do everything from a sad nature. Moods are like the weather report for an entire day. Like a forecast. Today will be bright and sunny. Tomorrow dark clouds no sunshine.

THOUGHTS-   Thought's are ourselves thinking inwardly (that is in our minds).Thought's are secondary and affections are primary. Thoughts are basically thinking from ones affections. Feelings are the beginning of the thought process (That is we come into thinking about things based on how we feel). Feelings give rise to thoughts and the thoughts manifests ones concerns about what we are feeling or about how we feel as to any given subject. Thoughts are also mental images of what we desire to do or say. Sometimes our thoughts seem to be hidden from us or lost, because we ignore the affections from whence those thoughts came. Thoughts are like the definitions of the word we are feeling. Feelings use thoughts as a means to be known. Without feelings there can be no thoughts to express what one is feeling. Thought's are like sensors reacting from the power source to whatever crosses in front of it. If there is no power there is nothing to sense. So thoughts and feelings act as one, just as love goes forth it is converted into ideas of pleasant thoughts by which it intelligently communicates itself to others. Feelings are the origins of the formation of thoughts in the mind. These are received in the brain by which impulses are sent throughout the body. Thoughts and feelings are thereby one with the body. This becomes a mind and body relationship. Thoughts become what we speak and feelings become what we express or act out in the body. Thus spiritual things use natural things to communicate to each other in a natural world.

MEMORY- is a mental collection of all things done or experienced as to one's life. It should be understood that there is an internal memory and an external memory. The one most common to man is external memory, which as was said above is a collection of all things done or experienced as to one's physical life. However, internal memory or memories of the spirit are the states of the mind in relation to the things done or experienced in one's life. This has more to do with the uncountable thoughts and affections that stem from and are in accordance with the nature of one's life as to the things done and experienced in the body.

RATIONALITY- is a higher thought process that is based on one's ability to think or reason concerning things reflected upon. It should also be understood that there are two states of rationality, one natural the other spiritual. Natural rationality is reason based on our five senses. It also has to do with the laws of physics and all other sciences that study to explain how things work as to the natural universe.

SPIRITUAL LAWS

The system or structure for how things work is called law and order. Laws originate in respect to order. Order is a chronological way of how things work. There are moral laws based on morality. Such as respect, behavior and honesty towards others as well as ourselves. There are civil laws based on legal matters involving disputes about property and also civil behavior as to what one says or does to another. There are natural laws such as the Laws of physics, the Law of gravity and the Law of probability. There's biology, which is the study of all living things as to their classification, physiology and chemistry and there are many more. Lastly, there are spiritual laws or laws of the mind. These laws transcend all time and space. They are beyond all moral and civil laws. For those laws has to do with how one presents himself to others through speech and actions of the body.

The state of the mind is dependent on things that affect the mind. In general and in particular the mind is affected and displays this by various emotions that come upon us when we see or hear bad things or good things. It is the life of the mind that reacts to things we see or hear in the body. The general states of our mind are constantly surrounded by spirits. Some of these spirits are not as present as others are at times, but they are always there being accepted or rejected by the life of the person. When something bad happens, the mind gravitates to the affections that are more like its own in nature. Consequently, when something bad happens some become angry others become sad some even become happy depending on the nature of one's mind as to its quality of life, so that the particular state of mind as to sadness is communicated to the body and expresses itself by tears and or facial expressions of sadness. Once the person's spirit is done with grieving they cast off the spirit of sadness and return or receive a better spirit as to their state of mind before the event happened. It should be understood that we draw spirits to ourselves. One should keep aware of his own state of mind so that he does not draw to himself spirits that are not of a good quality of life. Those who are regenerated and are said to have the Holy Spirit are surrounded by what are called angelic spirits who are of a like nature and quality of the man himself and who by the Lord assist him in his daily living. Other spirits are called evil spirits they inspire sadness, anger, hatred and all other negative feelings into the person. So if we *"watch and pray"* we can avoid attracting spirits that are opposed to heavenly affections. And even when we can't avoid them, if we look to the Lord He can keep them from overwhelming us and even cast them away from us. For we all at times experience these negative affections being that we are tempted many times daily by evil spirits to think or act in a negative way. But when we are down He picks us up. When we are lonely He suddenly can make us feel that we are not alone. He changes what is evil to good. He makes the darkness light before us. For evil spirits you see desire to rule the man, but the Lord is constantly surrounding those who are born again with a host of angels who more directly than us are filled and led of the Holy Spirit.

There is nothing more real about you than your spirit. Everything actual or real about you is in your spirit. That which is spiritual is what is real. Spiritual laws originate from the spiritual world. When one looks to do good from a life of good (that is from a desire for genuine good) he is surrounded by good in the spiritual world for the affections of good are spiritual and they come forth from there. Consequently, the works of the body that he does are from and in genuine good. But when one is not in genuine good he is in conditional good, which means they are only interested in doing good works when they can get something out of it. This goodness would be called infatuated good. Like a neon light compared to a candle light. They both cause life like effects outwardly, but inwardly one is made of pure fire and the other is not. It should be understood that both are considered spiritual, it's just that one is of a genuine quality and the other is not. The former can be called spiritual (heavenly) and the latter carnal (infernal), but they both are states of the life of the mind which are made up of spiritual substances, for the thoughts and affections of the mind are immaterial (that is spiritual) and not physical.

In the spiritual world spiritual laws are in effect. The mind as to genuine good contains within it unconditional joy, peace and contentment. It genuinely looks to the good of others as well as themselves without need of a reward or self merit. The more one desires to do genuine good to others the more he is opened to genuine good for himself. For spiritual laws are based on a person's state of mind toward others as well as himself and not on how much one does or posses physically for himself or others.

A PARALLEL WORLD

The parallel world we are talking about is a world within another world, but connected in a way that the one could not survive without the other. An analogy of this would be the fact that the body has external parts such as skin, nails, hair, teeth and the like that apparently covers the body. Then there are the internal parts of the body such as the organs, nerves, bones, muscles and the like. We all know that a person although with all his external parts could not exist or survive without his internal parts. So the external and the internal have a kind of parallel existence. The external parts and the internal parts hold the person together and make them whole. The internal parts without the external can in some measure survive but not for long. For the internal would become unstable due to the absence of the external by which the internal was properly adapted to be able to work through to get work done. This is the same way by which the two parallel worlds are situated.

The internal is called the spiritual world and the external is called the natural world. The spiritual world is the cause of the existence of the natural world. The Divine itself is the cause of the existence of the spiritual world and through this the natural world, thus creation. Life from the Divine flows into the natural world through the spiritual world, creating suitable forms of life from that one life variously received. If the forms become unsuitable for life then it is said that the person dies. For the form is made for the reception of life. There are also degrees of life from that one life variously received. The lowest are called inanimate

or the mineral kingdom, the second are things that grow or the plant kingdom, the third are animate or the animal kingdom where man is in the highest degree of that one life that is variously received. The Divine alone is life and all life flows in from Him. All others are receivers of life according to the nature and disposition as to what they were created.

It should be also understood that when we say the spiritual world we mean heaven and hell. Good and pleasant things in creation come from the earth being in harmony with heaven, but evil and harmful things come from the earth being in harmony with hell. Therefore when man disobeyed God it is said that the earth brought forth thorns and thistles. Man had dominion over the earth, so when man had let these things into his spirit, the earth in response brought forth those things which dominated in man. Before this it was the Lord who dominated in man, therefore the earth was in good standing, for mans dominion over the earth was in and from good."Thy will be done on earth as it is in heaven". But when sin dominated in man, it began to be done on earth as it is in hell and the earth brought forth evils of every kind (Thorns and thistles and the like) in correspondence to the nature of the dominion in which now dominated in man.

THE TRINITY

The doctrine of the trinity is very important. Although the bible does not clearly state word for word that there are three Gods in the trinity. It has been widely accepted in Christendom that this is the case. This in part is due to some scriptures understood in a certain way. The other idea's of the trinity that most have is that each one is God and is independent of the other (that is that they are their own Person, but are in agreement as one). Each God is from eternity, and is omnipresent, omniscient and omnipotent. Also that no one in the trinity is greater than the other, but recognized as coeternal. Most of what I'm saying can be validated and found in the Athanasian Creed which has been accepted as the creed of the trinity throughout the protestant churches. Also each God is considered to be a person or individual and that no one in the trinity is before the other or after the other. Consequently they are considered to be three as one. Here is a majority portion of that Creed.

Athanasian Creed

1. Whosoever will be saved, before all things it is necessary that he hold the catholic faith;

2. Which faith except every one do keep whole and undefiled, without doubt he shall perish everlastingly.

3. And the catholic faith is this: That we worship one God in Trinity, and Trinity in Unity;

4. Neither confounding the persons nor dividing the substance.

5. For there is one person of the Father, another of the Son, and another of the Holy Spirit.

6. But the Godhead of the Father, of the Son, and of the Holy Spirit is all one, the glory equal, the majesty coeternal.

7. Such as the Father is, such is the Son, and such is the Holy Spirit.

8. The Father uncreated, the Son uncreated, and the Holy Spirit uncreated.

9. The Father incomprehensible, the Son incomprehensible, and the Holy Spirit incomprehensible.

10. The Father eternal, the Son eternal, and the Holy Spirit eternal.

11. And yet they are not three eternals but one eternal.

12. As also there are not three uncreated nor three incomprehensible, but one uncreated and one incomprehensible.

13. So likewise the Father is almighty, the Son almighty, and the Holy Spirit almighty.

14. And yet they are not three almighties, but one almighty.

15. So the Father is God, the Son is God, and the Holy Spirit is God;

16. And yet they are not three Gods, but one God.

17. So likewise the Father is Lord, the Son Lord, and the Holy Spirit Lord;

18. And yet they are not three Lords but one Lord.

19. For like as we are compelled by the Christian verity to acknowledge every Person by himself to be God and Lord;

20. So are we forbidden by the catholic religion to say; There are three Gods or three Lords.

21. The Father is made of none, neither created nor begotten.

22. The Son is of the Father alone; not made nor created, but begotten.

23. The Holy Spirit is of the Father and of the Son; neither made, nor created, nor begotten, but proceeding.

24. So there is one Father, not three Fathers; one Son, not three Sons; one Holy Spirit, not three Holy Spirits.

25. And in this Trinity none is before or after another; none is greater or less than another.

26. But the whole three persons are coeternal, and coequal.

27. So that in all things, as aforesaid, the Unity in Trinity and the Trinity in Unity is to be worshipped.

28. He therefore that will be saved must thus think of the Trinity.

29. Furthermore it is necessary to everlasting salvation that he also believe rightly the incarnation of our Lord Jesus Christ.

30. For the right faith is that we believe and confess that our Lord Jesus Christ, the Son of God, is God and man.

31. God of the substance of the Father, begotten before the worlds; and man of substance of His mother, born in the world.

32. Perfect God and perfect man, of a reasonable soul and human flesh subsisting.

33. Equal to the Father as touching His Godhead, and inferior to the Father as touching His manhood.

34. Who, although He is God and man, yet He is not two, but one Christ.

35. One, not by conversion of the Godhead into flesh, but by taking of that manhood into God.

36. One altogether, not by confusion of substance, but by unity of person.

37. For as the reasonable soul and flesh is one man, so God and man is one Christ;

The confusion many, many people have with this is that, if they are considered individuals or that if each God is considered to be his own person. How could they be one in essence? We are told in the Athanasian Creed in section:19

19. For like as we are compelled by the Christian verity to acknowledge every Person by himself to be God and Lord;

20. So are we forbidden by the catholic religion to say; there are three Gods or three Lords".

So here we see three persons acknowledged as three Gods. However, it says, it is not permitted to say that there are three Gods. It may be because the bible does not mention or use the term three Gods either. In fact it clearly states the opposite such as in, 1Tim 2:5
"For there is one God and one mediator between God and man, the man Christ Jesus," Also in Isaiah 45:2
"Tell ye, and bring them near; yea, let them take counsel together: who hath declared this from ancient times? Who hath told it from that time? Have not I the Lord? And there is no God else beside me; a just God and a savior; there is none beside me".

Let us take a look at the trinity as three Gods in one. Throughout all creation there is a sought of trine, but none of them show an image of three persons as one. For in speaking of three persons, each person must have his own essence apart from another to be considered an individual. When we look at a tree, there are three essentials that are needed to make a tree. (For the sake of those who do not understand the word essence, it is the attribute or set of attributes that make an object or substance what it fundamentally is, and the word essential is that which something posses that is needed to retain its identity or existence.) The root, stem, and the branches are the three essentials that make one tree. So the Father, Son and Holy Spirit are three essentials that make one God, otherwise known as the Divine, Divine Human and The Divine Proceeding. These three together constitute one Divine in whom dwells a trinity of three divine operations. Therefore, because man was created in the image of God there also dwells in him a likeness of a trinity. The human body itself is divided into three sections. The head, upper body, and lower body altogether make one body. Are not the soul, spirit and body three essentials that make up the life of man? All throughout creation this is seen. Are there not three kingdoms that make one earth? These are the mineral kingdom, the plant kingdom and the animal kingdom. Even the atom is made of three essential components that make it an atom. The electron, proton and neutron. It's no wonder the number three is used to signify what is complete. For Christ rose in the three days, Jonah was three days in the belly of the whale, Peter denied Christ three times, Christ spoke to peter three times about feeding his sheep and lambs. Lastly it was said to baptize in the name of the Father, the Son and the Holy Spirit. It shows that there are three titles, but they are under one name, three essentials that makeup one essence, three operations, but one operator. So here it is. We may say there are three, but we know in essence there is only one.

The Holy Spirit

The Bible tells us in Jn 7:39 *"that the Holy Spirit was not yet, because Jesus was not yet glorified"*. Nowhere in the OT does it mention that the Holy Spirit spoke to anyone. Where the term holy spirit is used which are only three places in the OT, which are Ps. 51:11, Isaiah 63:10, and verse 11. They refer to the presence of God's holiness in their life and not to a third person of the trinity with them. In the OT whenever the Lord spoke to the prophets, it would always say that "the Word of the Lord came unto me", or "Thus saith the Lord", or especially when he moved upon them it would say "The spirit of the Lord" but never would it say that the Holy Spirit spoke to them or that the Lord spoke to them by the Holy Spirit as it does in the NT, for unless the Lord had been born there would've been no Holy Spirit for us to receive . This is because the Word tells us in John 7:39 *"But this spake he of the Spirit which they that believe on him should receive: For the Holy Ghost was not yet given; because that Jesus was not yet glorified."* Again, it is only because of Christ that the Holy Spirit is given. Therefore, the Word says in John 15:26 *"that the Lord Jesus Christ would send the Holy Spirit from the Father"*.

If the Holy Spirit was always from the beginning operating as another person of the God head and supposedly gave its hand in the creation of the universe and of mankind, why would it say that the Holy Spirit was not yet come? When it would have already been here? And if it was already here as another person of the God head he would have to be omnipresent, but yet Jesus says that He would send it to them and that they were even to wait for it. The bible also notes that when it came for the first time, it came like a mighty rushing wind which was its introduction into the world. Another question arises. Why would Jesus call the Holy Spirit He? By saying *"When He the Spirit of truth has come. He would reprove the world of sin"*. As if He was another person? The answer to this can be seen by whom the Holy Spirit is sent out, which according to scripture is the Lord, for that which is sent out from the Lord, and draws all to himself, is his Spirit. The Holy Spirit and because the operation of the Holy Spirit is from the Lord alone the Holy Spirit is therefore referred to as He. The Holy Spirit gives us all things that are in Christ. Therefore, in essence who else could the Holy Spirit come from? It is the spirit of Christ which in essence is Christ the Lord among us. In John 16:13 it says *"Howbeit when he, the Spirit of truth, is come, he will guide you into all truth: for he shall not speak of Himself; but whatsoever he shall hear, that shall he speak: and he will shew you things to come"* It is said that *"He shall not speak of Himself, but shall take of mine and show it unto you"*. The Holy Spirit, being a proceeding from the Father, does not speak of itself. Neither can it, for it proceeds from the Father. It is the communication and performance of those things that proceed from the Divine will of the Lord. That it does proceed from the Father the Lord himself say's in John 15:

26 *But when the Comforter is come, whom I will send unto you from the Father, even the Spirit of truth, which proceedeth from the Father, he shall testify of me:*

Since the Father and the Son are one. The Holy Spirit receives not just from the Father, but also from the Son as the Lord say's in John 16:

"14 He shall glorify me: for he shall receive of mine, and shall shew it unto you.

15 All things that the Father hath are mine: therefore said I, that he shall take of mine, and shall shew it unto you."

The reason why the Lord is speaking of Himself in the third person is because he would not be present with them anymore in the way they knew him, which was in his earthly body, but by another way he would be present with them *always even unto the end of the world*, not by his flesh, which was no more, but by his very own spirit which could be none other than the Holy Spirit which in essence is the Lord himself among them. However, because the body of Christ is one thing and the spirit of Christ is another. The Holy Spirit was identified as being sent by Jesus Christ into the hearts of all believers. This is why without the Holy Spirit, which is the spirit of Christ, no man can be saved, as it is written in Romans 8: 9 *"But ye are not in the flesh, but in the Spirit, if so be that the Spirit of God dwell in you. Now if any man have not the Spirit of Christ, he is none of his."* The Spirit of God and the Spirit of Christ are here used interchangeably, because they are one and the same. He that hath the Spirit of God has the Spirit of Christ and he that hath the Spirit of Christ has the Spirit of God which in this case is the same as having the Holy Spirit. As it is written in Ephesus 2:*18 "For through him we both have access by one Spirit unto the Father."*

The Lord's omnipresence, omniscience, and omnipotence among his creation are by his Holy Spirit. Before the Lords birth the Holy Spirit was known as the Spirit of God which was said in Gen 1:3 *to move upon the face of the waters.* Since the time of the coming of the Lord the Spirit of God has been identified as the Holy Spirit due to the fact that by God becoming a man, He has made his spirit adaptable to be received by all men for the sake of their salvation. Before this, salvation was by the Law, for the Spirit of God at that time was not receivable by men (for the sake of salvation) due to the mindset to which they had fallen. However, the Spirit of God was still able to be among them representatively by the institution of the Law and of the prophets which all looked to Christ. So that where the Law was limited through the flesh, Christ by the glorification of his resurrection was able to give us his Holy Spirit so that we would no longer serve the Law according to the flesh, but according to the Spirit. When the Lord told his disciples in Matt 28:26 *"Lo I am with you always even unto the end of the world"* It was clearly meant that by his Holy Spirit he would always be with them. The Lord as the Holy Spirit is among us for our reformation, regeneration, and vivification, purification from evils, justification and salvation. These in turn produce what are called the fruits of the Holy Spirit which are all effects of salvation and these are mentioned in Gal 5:20. These are of his Divine love which all consists of His salvation. As the Word says in 1 John 4:7 *"Beloved, let us love one another: for love is of God; and every one that loveth is born of God, and knoweth God."*

There are also those which are called the gifts of the Holy Spirit. Again this is the Lord among us as the Holy Spirit operating upon man and through men. These are to be found in 1 Corin 12. These are of his Divine Wisdom and consist of all things which assist in leading to salvation. They do not mean that one has salvation. It should be understood that "the gifts and calling of God are without repentance" (Rom 11:29). They are used to minister to the unsaved to assist in leading them to salvation as well as for the up building of faith of those who are saved.

These two, Divine Love and Divine Wisdom are two essentials of the Lords life, for He is Wisdom itself and Love Itself. These two are what are spiritually meant in Gen 1:26 when He says "Let us make man in our image after our likeness". For Divine Wisdom from which comes Divine truth is what reforms man and leads him to salvation. So long as man is being reformed he is not yet regenerated and is therefore only an image of God, for truths deals with the faculty of the understanding in man and not his will (that is unless man receives them into his will), for his will which is of his heart must be changed and this is done by him becoming born again of the truths which he is now learning. But once he has been regenerated which comes after he has received the truths of faith and lives after them from genuine love he then becomes a likeness of God. For an image is according to a likeness. Therefore to be an image of God is good, but to be a likeness of God is greater. An image refers to the life of those whose consciousness is convicted by the truths of faith. A likeness refers to the life of those who are in a perception of the truths of faith from the good of love. So the Phrase *"let us make man in our image after our likeness"* in Gen 1:26 is referring to the life of the Lords Divine wisdom in operation upon mans understanding as to the truths of faith and the life of the Lords Divine Love in operation upon mans will as to the good of love both of which are God. Divine love and wisdom are distinguishably one in the Lord. That is, they are two divine essentials of the Divine Life itself. The name of God here in Hebrew is Elohim, (here Elohim' governs the <u>singular</u> Hebrew verb ''*amer*' (Strong's # 559)), which is God's name in a singular sense, but the words *"let us make man in our image after our likeness" refers to God in a plural sense,* which again is referring to the two essentials of the one God in man's life. Which are the life of the Divine Wisdom from which comes all spiritual truth and the life of Divine love from which comes all spiritual good.

Now as all truth which is from God is God himself among us and as we know His Word is what is true it is said in John 1:1 *"In the beginning was the Word and the Word was with God and the Word was God"*, for all though it speaks as if there are two by the saying *"and the Word was with God"* yet in essence they are one for it says that *"the Word was God"*. And as there are many Divine truths in the Word all of which are God and from God among men, it is said *"Let us make man in our image"*, for there are infinite truths in God

each of which is God among us that together forms us into that one image of God himself. For God is truth itself or the Word itself. And every truth or Word from him is Himself among men in reference to some particular truth that is for the continual preservation and salvation of the life of man. For it tells us that since the beginning *"The Word was God"* and since the Word is God and God is a spirit, every truth from the Word is God in spirit among us for the sake of our reformation, regeneration and salvation. The words that God spoke which were *"Let us make man in our image after our likeness"* are therefore referring to all the truths of faith each of which creates man into Gods own image. For each truth is god creating man into the one image of God Himself. This is why the words *"let us make man in our image after our likeness" are* employed here. And, because there is only one God in whom are all Divine truths, it is said thereafter in the singular in Gen 1:27 *"So God created man in his own image, in the image of God created he him;"* In the scriptures it said that we are gods in psalms 81:6 were it reads,
"I have said, ye are gods; and all of you are children of the most High".
 And this is confirmed by Christ in John 10:34
"Jesus answered them, is it not written in your law, I said, ye are gods?"
Not that they were gods from themselves, but that they were called gods because of the truths of faith

which were with them and in them of which they had received from the Word of God, for it goes on to say " and all of you are children of the most High". All the truths of faith taken individually are what are called gods, for they each and all are used to create man into the image of the one God. And all those who receive these truths are likewise called gods for all truths taken individually as well as those who receive them are all images of God from whom they come. An analogy of this would be found in the stars and in the sun. The stars taken individually are little suns, for they are in the image of the Sun of our solar system. Yet each and all of them are in one universe, so each and all truths are in one God. The same holds true as to Divine love from which comes all spiritual good. For spiritual good is that by which man has love for spiritual truths. If these spiritual truths are not in his heart, then they are only head knowledge of which alone he cannot be saved until they becomes matters of his heart, for then they are of his life. For the two make one life. The life of mans understanding receives the truths of faith and the life of mans will receives the good of love which are matters of the heart pertaining to all the truths of faith. For spiritual good and truth from the Lord is the Lord Himself and the Lord as to these is infinite, that is without end. This is how man can go from glory to glory or climb to deeper and deeper depths in the Lord.

Since the time of creation man has fallen from the place in which the Lord had created them and therefore for the sake of mans preservation and salvation the Lord Himself needed to become man so that by the Spirit of his man life called the Holy Spirit, He would be adaptable to the reception of all men that is to whomsoever would believe on him and thus be saved. This is why after his glorification it tells us in John 20:22,
"he breathed on them, and saith unto them, Receive ye the Holy Ghost:"
This is why the Word says there is no salvation in any other. For without the Lord becoming human there would be no Spirit of Christ by which all humans are saved who believe on the Son of God, for as it is written in Romans 8:9 *"Now if any man have not the Spirit of Christ, he is none of his"*.
And because the Spirit of Christ and the Holy Spirit are one and the same, it was again said by Paul in Ephesians 2:
18 *For through him we both have access by one Spirit unto the Father.*

THEOLOGICAL DISCUSSIONS

THEOLOGICAL DISCUSSIONS

1

I am the way the truth and the life

John 14:6, 7 "I am the Way the Truth and the Life no man cometh unto the Father but by me. If you had known me you should have known my Father also. And from henceforth you know him, and have seen him".

To Brian: Understand that what is in God is also with God, so Jesus is God and is from God. Everything in the mind is with the mind and consists of it and comes forth from it and is extended to others. They are essentially one and the same. Everything in the mind is called God the Father and everything that goes forth from that mind and is extended to others is called the Son. This is how He only could be the Savior, because in essence He is God and being from God He leads us back to God.

The oneness of the Father and Son

Notes: It is said "And from henceforth ye know him and have seen him". That is, they now know the quality and characteristics of the Father by knowing and observing or seeing the life of Christ. For Apostle John says in
1 John 1:2

For the life was3w manifested, and we have seen it, and bear witness, and shew unto you that eternal life, which was with the Father, and was manifested unto us;

In John1:1

"And the Word was with God and the Word was God" *That is, the same Word that was with God was and is God.*

Therefore, the Father who is God and God who is the Word is Jesus Christ manifested in the flesh. Otherwise, according to the Athanasian Creed the Son who was with the Father from eternity could only manifest himself in the flesh and not the Father due to the fact that the Father is not the Son (That is He is another person distinguished from the Son). It being said in the Athanasian Creed that they are one does not dismiss the fact that it also says the Son is one person and the father is another. If there is one person of the Father and another person of the Son, they cannot be one and the same.

2

God so Loved the World

God so loved the world that He sent his only begotten son into the world, that we might live through him. 1 john 4:9

To Brian: John tells us that God is Love, but the Son who is called the Word was sent forth to accomplish Loves will. Consequently the Word is God as to Divine wisdom. For it is said he sends out his Word and it does not return to him void. Also the scripture says our God is a consuming fire. And what does fire send forth, but light. This is why He say's "I am the light of the world'. The Fire is Divine Love the Light from it is Divine wisdom that goes forth carrying love (heat) with it in all that it goes out to accomplish. This is the answer to all your thoughts about wisdom as to who possessed it and who brought it forth and more.

Divine wisdom itself is God and not another person

Notes: In proverbs 8, it speaks of Wisdom as if it were another person. When, nevertheless God is Wisdom itself. It states in verse 22 "that the Lord possessed me in the beginning of his ways before his works of old."*It is written as if it was another person, when nevertheless God is omniscient. That is, all knowing. Further, concerning wisdom it says*"

23 I was set up from everlasting, from the beginning, or ever the earth was.

24 When there were no depths, I was brought forth; when there were no fountains abounding with water.

25 Before the mountains were settled, before the hills was I brought forth:

26 While as yet he had not made the earth, nor the fields, nor the highest part of the dust of the world.

27 When he prepared the heavens, I was there: when he set a compass upon the face of the depth:

28 When he established the clouds above: when he strengthened the fountains of the deep:

29 When he gave to the sea his decree, that the waters should not pass his commandment: when he appointed the foundations of the earth:

30 Then I was by him, as one brought up with him: and I was daily his delight, rejoicing always before him;

Anyone can see that wisdom is an attribute of God himself and that it is not another person. The same is written in St John 1:1 concerning the Word where it says "the Word was with God". *As if it were another person, but then he goes on to say* "the Word was God". *God's Word and*

Wisdom are said to be with God, because he uses them for the sake of others. When nevertheless God is the Word and God is wisdom, for God is the omniscient one.

3

Mystery of the Father and the Son

Scripture says *"it is the spirit that quickeneth the flesh profits nothing"." The words I speak unto you are spirit and Life"*. Also *"He is the image of the invisible God"* col 2:15.

To James: The body is indeed a representation and an image, but the Life of the body is the actual thing or is the essential thing and this, my friend is God alone. The body was only used to be among men and make divine his human so that he might also save all humanity by it. After his glorification this was accomplished, for he had put off the limitations of the body into which he was born through Mary. This is why he was able to suffer as other men, because although he was not yet fully Divine as to his body, (because he had not yet had been glorified) He was still able to draw from His Divine from whence came all power. He drew his strength from the Divine which was within Him and this he called the Father and prayed to him as if he was another person, for the Divine itself unlike the nature of his humanity which he received from Mary is omnipresent, Omnipotent and all knowing, when all along he was the Father, but only weak as to the flesh. "The spirit is willing, but the flesh is weak."Consequently after His glorification when his body became one with his Divine He said "All power is given unto me in heaven and in earth." That is He came into all power after the glorification of his body. One must first understand the doctrine of the nature of God and the doctrine of the Holy Scriptures in order to understand the mystery of God and the Son.

The Doctrine of the Holy Scriptures

Notes: *The doctrine of the Holy Scriptures is concerning the style in which the Word was written. For men, it is written literally according to how things appear in this world. For men see and hear all things in this world according to how they are presented in nature. For example,* in psalm 113:3, and psalm 50:1 *as well as in other places the bible says that the sun rises and goes down, when nevertheless it never moves. It is written that way according to how it appears in nature. It is also written according to attributes and characteristics that are relatable to men, in order* *that they may understand and relate to the Word in a natural way, for men are first born natural and must be aided until he becomes spiritual and the Word does this from beginning to end. For example in* Gen 2:2, it says that God had rested on the seventh day, from all the work that he had made, *when nevertheless he is Omnipotent and never needs rest. This is said in the scriptures, because man naturally needs rest and can relate to getting rest, but for God it says* "He never sleeps or slumbers" *(these words are used, because man can relate to sleeping and slumbering), besides the fact he is constantly leading and guiding us and always watching over us as well as over his creation. Whereby, if he were to rest from all this, the universe would collapse, for he constantly supplies the power that is needed for it to continue and this in such a way that if it is to continue he could never rest.*

4

Christ is God and Savoir

To Brian and James: Nothing you have written addresses what I have given. I had already read all your comments before that is why I responded. The Jews were also angry with him, because he made himself equal to YHWH, only because they could not understand anything beyond the flesh. The natural intellectual mind is one thing and the spiritual intellect is another. "If I tell you earthly things and ye believe not how shall ye understand heavenly things". John 3:12. For as the Father hath life in himself, so hath He given to the Son to have Life in Himself: And hath given him to execute judgment also, because he is the Son of man. John 5:26, 27. You fail to understand also that He is the only begotten Son of God, for he was conceived of the Holy Spirit and not Joseph. His spirit was YHWH the Father (who hath life in himself) and his body was the Son (who was given life in himself) who cannot see that in essence they are one and the same. What is a body without its spirit, but a dead one? Again *the flesh profiteth nothing it is the Spirit that quickeneth" John 6:63.* Blindness comes by substituting natural thinking for spiritual thinking, whereby no spiritual truth can be seen.

"Though I bear record of myself yet my record is true: For I know whence I came, and whither I go: but ye cannot tell whence I come and whither I go. Ye judge after the flesh I judge no man. And yet if I judge my judgment is true: for I am not alone, but I and the Father who sent me."John 8:14-16.

The body does nothing of itself except by the spirit. There is a spirit of man and there is the spirit of God. Mans spirit is given along with his body at creation and is continually given through procreation. But YHWH spirit existed before He put on a body. This why Yeshua say's in *John 8:23 "That ye are from beneath: I am from above: ye are of this world: I am not of this world".* Again, *before Abraham was I am" John 8:58.* There are not two Gods, but one or else how can Yeshua be called *"Everlasting Father"* by the Prophet Isaiah. This is why he says often that the Father hath sent me. The Father is the selfsame God as to Divine Love and Son as to Divine wisdom. It is the Divine Wisdom that is sent out to save and to do all things that Love sends him to do. *"I am the light of the world: he that followeth me shall not walk in darkness, but shall have the light of life. John 8:12.* The Life (The Father) is Divine Love which sends out the light (The Son) which is Divine wisdom to lead all men back unto himself. Who can have a heart without lungs or thoughts without will? As a man thinks in his heart so is he. So as the Divine Wisdom "Yeshua" is from Divine Love "YHWH" the two make one life. And in essence are one and the same.

5

The representation of Israel and Judah!

To James: Just as Christ as a child went to Egypt and then was called out, so did Israel go into Egypt and so likewise was called out. This is because Israel depicted Christ representatively, as did everything else that also pertained to their Laws. But spiritually speaking Israel signified the spiritual progress of the establishment of the church that was to come as well as did Christ which was symbolized by them coming forth out of Egypt as a child. As for Judah That ruleth with God and is faithful with the saints, remember *" a ruler shall come forth out of Judah to rule over Israel whose going forth have been from of old, from everlasting"* Mic 5:2. Again this is in reference to God himself as to his celestial qualities which are in respect to his Divine love from which goes forth his Divine Wisdom (the Son) to rule over His people Israel and He is faithful among the saints. And indeed He also is called the faithful and true witness in Revelation.

All things written in the Word have a spiritual meaning

Notes: Because the Word is the Lord all things in it treat of him. It also treats of things in him, such as the divine qualities and characteristics of life that are with him and are in him and in essence are him. For what is in a man is what makes the man, so likewise what is in God is what makes him God. 1 John 4:7 tells us that God is Love, Jude 1:25 Tells us that God is wise. *And because the quality of the life of God is Divine, all things of which that Divine life consists of are also divine. Therefore his love and his wisdom are called Divine Love and Divine Wisdom, and because He is the Divine itself, He his Love itself and Wisdom itself and these constitute life itself. Now these qualities and characteristics are with him as well as in him, for it is these thwings that define him as being God. What else would the name of God be without the divine attributes and qualities of life and characteristics wherein it consists? It would be like a shell with no content or like a body without the organs that constitute life such as the heart, lungs, liver and so forth. Without these He would be nothing, but with them, they are what make him God and because the word is God and from God it treats of God.*

God is a spirit. Therefore, the Word must be understood spiritually in order to know who God truly is. Understanding the Word literally or as it is written is not enough. For it is like judging someone according to the look of their face and not according to the discerning of the interiors of their mind. For we all know that judging according to how someone looks is according to appearances, but judging according to the discernment of the interiors of the mind is spiritual and therefore to know them as to their spirit is to truly know them as to who they really are. Therefore the words of the Bible must be understood spiritually in order to know who God truly is as he is in himself.

6

Yeshua is YHWH in the flesh!

To Brian: You could not have mentioned a better scripture *"behold a virgin shall conceive, and bear a son, and shall call his NAME IMMANUEL"*. Because the Word is God all the Holy Scriptures must bear reference to him. Because the Word is with God and from God the Word is first Divine, then spiritual (that is among angels in heaven), then earthly (that is among men). Oh what do you think? That Yeshua is the son of David as the Jews thought, but then He corrected them and said *"What think ye of Christ? Whose son is he? They say unto him the son of David. He saith unto them, how then doth David in spirit call him Lord, saying. The Lord said unto my Lord; Sit down on my right hand until I make thine enemies thy footstool? If David then calls him Lord how is he his son? And no man was able to answer him a word, neither durst any man from that day forth ask him any more questions"* Matt 22:42-46.

All scripture in its genuine sense which is spiritual bear's reference to Yeshua being YHWH, coming from YHWH and physically becoming a Man as YHWH and that man was called Yeshua, especially the Hebrew bible. For this was dictated by YHWH himself. *Dan 7:13-14,27 SAY'S"* <u>*I SAW AND BEHOLD ONE LIKE THE SON OF MAN CAME WITH CLOUDS OF HEAVEN*</u>, *AND THERE WAS GIVEN HIM DOMINION, AND GLORY, AND A KINGDOM, THAT ALL PEOPLES AND NATIONS, AND LANGUAGES MAY WORSHIP HIM: HIS DOMINION IS AN EVERLASTING DOMINION, WHICH SHALL NOT PASS AWAY, AND HIS KINGDOM THAT WHICH SHALL NOT BE DESTROYED: AND ALL DOMINIONS SHALL WORSHIP HIM AND OBEY HIM"*. If you know your Bible you know that Yeshua mentioned the same things about himself in *Matthew 24:30 AND THEN SHALL APPEAR* <u>*THE SIGN OF THE SON OF MAN IN HEAVEN*</u>: *AND THEN ALL THE TRIBES OF THE EARTH SHALL MORN,* <u>*AND THEY SHALL SEE THE SON OF MAN COMING IN THE CLOUDS OF HEAVEN*</u> *WITH POWER AND GREAT GLORY*, or what? Is this not enough for you? To whom belongs all worship from all peoples? Is it not YHWH? But Yeshua is YHWH who has already come and will return again as Daniel the Hebrew teaches upon the clouds of heaven. There are too many scriptures for me to recount suffer this to suffice. All the kings of Israel and its priests represented the Lord in one aspect or another. Why do you think they were said to be holy, surely not because they were, for they were more than all others idolaters, avaricious, and after all the miracles that was showed to them coming out of Egypt they were still unfaithful and YHWH wanted to destroy them all and start again. No they were not holy, but they could represent a holy people that were to come and also represent the qualities that were of YHWH and from YHWH in Yeshua and unto all those who would believe on him and do his commandments. Upon whose heart the law was written. Thereby they would know how to love and show love and how to entreat one another in righteousness as to all things that we do in this life. These videos only confirm Yeshua's Identity as to what he is and what he can and will be to all as to name and characteristics of life, for none can be worship except YHWH and YHWH is Yeshua who has come. *"Thou Bethlehem Ephrata, little as thou art to be among the thousands of Judah, out of thee shall come forth unto me that is to be ruler in Israel, and whose goings forth are from of old, from the days of eternity. He shall stand and feed in the strength of YHWH"* Micah 5:2,4. I suppose you think this speaks of someone else also. No my friend the Word is God and therefore is concerning him alone as to His Divinity and the spiritual quality of the life of those who are and will be of his kingdom, or what? Who is from of old, from the days of eternity, but YHWH alone. This is not hard at all, if you are willing to see it. It is plain and before you. Can you not see it? *"For thy maker is thy husband; the Lord of host is his name: and thy redeemer the Holy one of Israel: The God of the whole earth shall he be called" Isaiah 54:5.*

7

Christ reveals himself in all the scriptures

To James: *"Then Yeshua said unto them o fools, and slow of heart to believe all that the prophets have spoken. Ought not Christ to have suffered these things, and enter into his glory? And beginning at Moses and all the prophets, he expounded unto them in all the scriptures the things concerning himself." Luke 24:25-27. Also "And Yeshua said unto them, these are the words I spoke unto you while I was yet with you, that all things must be fulfilled, which were written in the law of Moses, and in the Prophets, and in the*

psalm, concerning me. Then he opened their understanding, that they might understand the scriptures. Luke 24:44-45.
The literal sense of the word was written for natural minded men. For example the bible say's the sun rises and sets and goes down. Obviously this is false, but for natural minded men (which is what everyone is born into) this appears to be true when looking at a sun rise. The whole bible is written in this manner and unless Yeshua opens our understanding as it says above namely by the spirit of truth, no man can understand the Word as it is in its genuine sense. And if I may say, Christ slain before the foundation of the world is referring to the end of the Old Testament by his death and the beginning of the New by his resurrection and ascension. It simply means that he had to be slain before there could be an establishment of the new era or testament that now is. But before creation there was only eternity and infinity. Time and space are products of creation and could not exist until then.

Natural rationality vs Spiritual rationality

Notes: There are two states of the mind. One is spiritual, and the other is natural. The natural mind thinks and reasons according to the five senses of the body and as these are in time and space which again are all in the natural world, ones thinking and reasoning and thus his mind are said to be natural when he thinks and reasons according to the state of these. The spiritual mind thinks and reasons according to what it senses in the spirit. The senses of the spirit are not like the five senses of the body which are natural and are of the natural world, but these are spiritual and are of the spiritual world and are not subject to time and space. Therefore ones thinking and reasoning according to this state are said to be of the spiritual mind. An example of the spiritual mind as well as of the spiritual world would be when Paul saw one caught up to the third heavens and he is said to have seen paradise and had heard things unlawful for a man to speak. The reason why it is said he heard things unlawful for a man to speak is because the understanding was not according to natural laws or laws of nature of which men are born into. For angels this is possible, but for men Paul says these words are unspeakable. Consequently, Paul saw things with spiritual eyes and heard things with spiritual ears in a spiritual state. Another example would be St John who according to the book of revelations was in the spirit on the Lords day and had seen and heard all things, not in the body, but in the spirit. By which the Lord gave him revelations and understanding concerning the end time. Yes all spiritual revelations and understanding of the Holy Scriptures comes by way of the Holy Spirit of whom it is said would lead us and guide us into all truth.

8

One trying to prove Yeshua is not YHWH as to scriptures

To Brian: I'm sorry, but I am not impressed. You are struggling to hard to UN-explain something clearly explained. I mean you are going out of your way to explain things, that yet and still you find inconclusive or unresolved yourself. How to you expect anyone else to not accept what is clearly written. I suppose you don't believe Yeshua was ever with YHWH in the beginning. "The Word was YHWH and the Word was with YHWH". "AND THE WORD WAS MADE FLESH". You said yourself Yeshua is the light beaming forth from YHWH. It is like light coming from a consuming fire. Obviously the light is not the fire, but what fire can you have without light? And what light can you have without fire? The light itself proves there is a source and the source is manifested by the light. The two are distinguishably one. You cannot have one without the other. Consequently, the two make one LIFE WHICH IS YHWH. What is the first creation of DIVINE FIRE is it not THE LIGHT? Does not THE LIGHT reveal what is in darkness? Does not THE LIGHT lead and guide our way into all TRUTH? Does not THE LIGHT instruct us and show us where we are to go? How we are to live?

"Yes *Yeshua is that LIGHT that lighth every man that cometh into the world. He was in the world, and the world was made by him, and the world knew him not."* John 1:9-10.

The Three Essentials of the Divine itself

Notes*: There are three titles given to one God who is known as the Father, the Son and the Holy Ghost. Just as there were three men who came to tell Abraham that Sarah was to have a child, and they were called Jehovah or Lord God for it is written in* Gen 18

1 And the Lord appeared unto him in the plains of Mamre: and he sat in the tent door in the heat of the day;

2 And he lift up his eyes and looked, and, lo, three men stood by him: and when he saw them, he ran to meet them from the tent door, and bowed himself toward the ground,

3 And said, My Lord, if now I have found favour in thy sight, pass not away, I pray thee, from thy servant:

Now as there were three that appeared to Abraham it is said that they spoke to him. Just as we have read places in the Word were the Father spoke, the Son spoke, and places were the Holy Spirit spoke, so that as three appeared to Abraham, so here also as to the three titles of the God head there appears three persons. Since the three titles signify three distinct operations, it was necessary that it should appear that three persons were involved as to the salvation of mankind, when nevertheless there was only one in essence, which is the Lord our God and savior who as the invisible Father from eternity became the visible Son in time who after his resurrection, ascension and glorification would never be known anymore as to the flesh, yet he said he would never leave them nor forsake them, that consequently by his spirit, which is called the Holy Spirit, He would always be among them. Everyone knows that the spirit of a man is not another person, but it is the very man himself apart from his body. So it is the same here with the Holy Spirit. The Holy Spirit is the Lord himself by means of which He dwells in us and leads us and guides us into all truth. It is the spirit of the man that is the real man himself, not the body which the Lord put off after his resurrection and ascension; neither could the Spirit be another person outside of himself. He himself said in John 6:63"What and if ye shall see the Son of man ascend up where he was before? 63 It is the spirit that quickeneth; the flesh profiteth nothing:

So it is now evident that the Lord did all things in his body by his Spirit which possessed the body, and that this Spirit was the Lord himself and not another person. However, for the sake of the representation of the three operations of the

Divine, three men appeared and it is said that they spoke to Abraham. For it is written in Gen18:
9 And they said unto him, where is Sarah thy wife? And he said, Behold, in the tent.

But because these three are in essence one person and not three persons it goes on to say that the Lord said and not they said. Gen 18:
13 And the Lord said unto Abraham, Wherefore did Sarah laughed, saying, Shall I of a surety bear a child, which am old?
14 Is anything too hard for the Lord? At the time appointed I will return unto thee, according to the time of life, and Sarah shall have a son.
15 Then Sarah denied, saying, I laughed not; for she was afraid. And he said, Nay; but thou didst laugh.
16 ¶And the men rose up from thence, and looked toward Sodom: and Abraham went with them to bring them on the way.
And because the Lord is one person in essence it is further said:
20 And the Lord said, because the cry of Sodom and Gomorrah is great, and because their sin is very grievous;
21 I will go down now, and see whether they have done altogether according to the cry of it, which is come unto me; and if not, I will know.
22 And the men turned their faces from thence, and went toward Sodom: but Abraham stood yet before the Lord.

So although there appeared three to represent the trinity, yet there is only one person in whom there is a trinity and He is the one and Self same person from the beginning.

9
Jesus is not God?

To Brian: *John 20:*
28 And Thomas answered and said unto him, My Lord and my God.
29 Jesus saith unto him, Thomas, because thou hast seen me, thou hast believed: blessed are they that have not seen, and yet have believed.
...If this was the case He would not have allowed Thomas to call him Lord God. Let alone commend him for saying such, but even rebuked him for needing to see him in order to believe that He was the Lord God.

But I would just like to add that Begotten Son does not mean adopted at all. The word begotten is like the word beget which is only used to identify someone's actual son or daughter, and actually means to procreate or produce from one's own loins. That is why who Christ is so significant.

Also if I may the Talmud is not the Torah so the explanation of Melchisedec from it is not at all admissible. As much as I do believe in the Hebrew bible I know for sure that the way it was written and how and what was written was by Divine order and that the Hebrew language itself as well as the culture related to it was designed to submit itself to that Divine Order so that the Scriptures might be understood in a particular way.

Now facebook is a hard way for us to get in depth about things, but there is that belief in the trinity of three Gods. This came from the Nicene Creed, as well as the Athanasian Creed, which followed. These creeds came about, because of the Doctrine of Arius who claimed that Christ was not divine in nature. Therefore, to keep this from being accepted throughout the Christendom they developed the two creeds mentioned, which according to their understanding made the Son another person from eternity as well as the Father as well as the Holy Spirit. But before all of these there was the Apostolic Doctrine. Which teaches that, "God is a Spirit (John 4:24), the Eternal One, the Creator of all things; and of course, of all men, thus making Him their Father (through creation). He is the FIRST and the LAST and beside Him there is no other. (Isaiah 44:6)

There was no God formed BEFORE Him, neither shall there be after Him.

"Jesus is the SON of God according to the flesh (Romans 1:3), and the very God Himself according to the Spirit. Jesus is the Christ (Matt 1:23); God made flesh (John 1:1-14); God manifested in the flesh (1 Tim 3:16); He which was, which is, and which is to come. THE ALMIGHTY (Rev 1:8; Isaiah 9:6).

and that the "The HOLY GHOST is not the third person in the Godhead, but rather the manifestation of the Spirit of God (the Creator), and of the resurrected Christ, coming to dwell in the hearts and lives of all men who will be obedient to the gospel, and the Comforter, Sustainer, and the Keeper (John 14:16-26; Romans 8:11).

So there are not three GODS, or persons, but three operations of ONE GOD who we know by the revealed face of God is Jesus Christ, God in Flesh."

Yes your right the Jews did not accept this. Even the His disciples had a hard time with it, but eventually accepted it.

John 16:

28 I came forth from the Father, and am come into the world: again, I leave the world, and go to the Father.

29 His disciples said unto him, Lo, now speakest thou plainly, and speakest no proverb.

That is, he came forth from the Divine by putting on a body from the Divine, and that he must return to his Divine with a new resurrected glorified body which had put off mortality and put on immortality, by changing his body into the same substance that His Divine is made of, by which the Divine and His body became one and the same. Therefore, after his resurrection he said *"all power is given unto me in heaven and in earth" Matt 26:28.*

And when He met Paul it was as a Divine Light from Heaven saying Paul, Paul why persecutest thou me.

Yeshua himself said to Satan. *"Thou shalt worship the Lord Thy God only".* So who will all worship as it is written in Daniel 7? Otherwise, why would you question the writers of the book of Hebrew written so long ago, unless they too had come to this understanding?

10

Scriptures showing Christ as God coming to Judge the earth

To John: The point is that Yeshua's birth is not a normal one, neither the prophecies concerning him and it cannot be normal if he is YHWH in the flesh. This is where Melchisedec comes in (unknown history. This means a lot as to Jewish culture) and also concerning David, if Yeshua was his son, David could not call Him Lord. So the Idea is not just about scripture spelling out virgin birth, but how it identifies him, whereby one can recognize what the nature of his birth had to be. Consequently coming from eternity into time, for

David is full of prophecies concerning YHWH coming to Judge the earth in *Psalm 96:*
13: For the Lord God cometh, he cometh to judge the earth: he shall judge the world with righteousness, and the people with his truth.
Micah 5:2
2 "But thou, Beth-lehem Ephratah, though thou be little among the thousands of Judah, yet out of thee shall one come forth unto me that is to be ruler in Israel; whose goings forth have been from of old, from everlasting."
Consequently coming from everlasting and then born in time is what the only begotten Son could possibly refer to.
Psalm 2:7
7 "I will declare the decree: the Lord hath said unto me, Thou art my Son; this day have I begotten thee."
The term begotten refers specifically to a direct descendant of the individual. "I have brought you forth", "I have bore you" and this meaning even carries further. To no other human could this be applied to other than the one brought forth by YHWH himself.
Psalm 89:25-27
"I will set his hand in the sea. He shall call me thou art my Father. I will make him my first born."
That is, his first and only human body born in time that came from himself.

To Mark: Elijah and St John had a similar signification. This is why John represented Elijah who was first to come to prepare the heart of the people for Yeshua. This is why they both wore a leathern girdle about their loins and other like clothing and things which indicated a similar representation that they served.

11

(Jewish) Understanding of Melchisedec as to OT laws

To John: "To the Jews, a traceable genealogy was of utmost importance, especially for the priesthood. If one could not prove his lineage he was barred from being a priest (Nehemiah 7:64). There is no recorded genealogy of Melchisedec. His descent was not important because his priesthood was not dependent on it. His lineage did not affect his right to the priesthood. The author went on to say in Hebrews 7:13-17 that the Law foretold of a day in which the Melchisedecian priesthood would arise again. Since under the Law of Moses the priesthood had to be of the Aaronic order, this gave evidence that the Law would one day be abolished in favor of a new covenant and consequently a new priesthood. The Law needed to be abolished because it demanded that the priests have their lineage through Aaron, not Melchisedec.

After the Law was abolished through Christ's death and the New Covenant was instituted with His blood, Jesus had no need to be in the lineage of Levi to serve as a priest of God. He could be of the stock of Judah and still be a priest under the order of Melchisedec, for there was no genealogical requirement for this order. The two priesthoods were of a different sort and order, serving two different purposes, at different times.

What does the phrase *"having neither beginning of days, nor end of life"* mean (Hebrews 7:3)? It could merely mean that the day of Melchisedec's birth and death are not recorded. This would be in stark contrast to other famous men of the Bible who births and deaths are recorded with great accuracy. It would also be in opposition to the importance of one's age under the Levitical and Aaronic priesthood, for under the Levitical priesthood one had to

prove their age so it could be determined whether or not they were too young or too old to serve as a priest. The Aaronic priests could not begin to serve as a priest until they were twenty-five years old, and had to retire when they reached the age of fifty (Numbers 4:1-3, 22-23, 35, 43; 8:24-25). Age was very important to the Aaronic priesthood, but not to Melchisedec's. He served as a priest for life."

I just think that this is pointing to the very essence of who Christ is as to the virgin birth. However, if our agreement does not go that far, I feel we at least do agree on the fact that Christ is called after the order of Melchisedec as King and Priest unto God Most High. Indeed the understanding of Melchisedec seems to be a much involved one as to Jewish culture.

The Representation of Christ by Melchisedec the Priest

Notes: Now Melchisedec who was said to have no beginning and no end of days. Neither, father or mother, but was considered Priest unto the Most High God, represented Christ. This is explained by Paul in Heb 7 from beginning to end, but more specifically in Heb 7:15-17 were it say's "15 And it is yet far more evident: for that after the similitude of Melchisedec there ariseth another priest,
16 Who is made, not after the law of a carnal commandment, but after the power of an endless life.
17 For he testifieth, Thou art a priest for ever after the order of Melchisedec."
In Heb 7:2-3 it says
"2 To whom also Abraham gave a tenth part of all; first being by interpretation King of righteousness, and after that also King of Salem, which is, King of peace;
3 Without father, without mother, without descent, having neither beginning of days, nor end of life;

but made like unto the Son of God; abideth a priest continually."

Anyone who reads these things concerning Melchisedec, must needs understand that these things were said in order that he should represent or signify Him who is from above who actually is without Father or mother, nor beginning of days, nor end of life and not that Melchisedec was without father or mother, without descent, having neither beginning or end of days, nor end of life, for he came into existence when he was born the same as all men are. However, info on when he was born and the genealogy of his birth as well as some other things were left out in order that He should represent Christ to come. For as was said above in the discussion, when the genealogy of one such as a priest is left out as it was with Melchesedec to whom Abraham paid tithes of which God permitted, they have no where to place him as to his order so consequently God willing that he should represent a higher order to come provided that this should be. Whereby, according to the Jewish laws and culture for priests this was seen as messianic prophecy.

Everyone needs to know and understand the power that spiritual representations possessed before the coming of Christ. For even Adam was a figure of Christ. The Word of the Lord was written in such a way that everything in it bears a representation to something spiritual. That the word is the Lord and that on this account it is holy containing innumerable arcane is confirmed in 2 Peter 1:20-21 says

"20 Knowing this first, that no prophecy of the scripture is of any private. interpretation.
21 For the prophecy came not in old time by the will of man: but holy men of God spake as they were moved by the Holy Ghost." *It may be hard to believe, but everything and everyone and even every place written of in the scriptures is representative of spiritual things. All spirituality comes from the Divine spiritual and therefore the spiritual sense of the Word bares reference to the Lord and all things from him, such as spiritual love, joy and peace and those who have these are of his spiritual Kingdom and have spiritual life. However, in the Word were evil is spoken of such as when Cain killed Abel as well as all other evil events that are written in the word, they are opposite to the Lord and to all things that are from him for these bares reference to the Devil and all things from him, such as hatred, revenge and cruelty, which again is spiritual, but this is of spiritual death.*

12

Christ the spiritual head of Moses and the Prophets

To James: Sorry I was very busy too!
Yes I know that Moses face did shone, but this was not a transfiguration at all. This was simply an effect of the Word itself upon Moses face. He was not aware of this at all. This was due to YHWH (Divine Wisdom) who is the Word itself talking as it were face to face with Moses. The effect of this caused Moses face to shine. This was simply an effect, not a transfiguration. For his face remained Shoned (glowing) when he came down from the mountain. As it says:

Exodus 34:29

¶And it came to pass, when Moses came down from mount Sinai with the two tables of testimony in Moses' hand, when he came down from the mount, that Moses wist not that the skin of his face shone while he talked with him. Also

33 And till Moses had done speaking with them, he put a vail on his face.

34 But when Moses went in before the Lord to speak with him, he took the vail off, until he came out. And he came out, and spake unto the children of Israel that which he was commanded.

35 And the children of Israel saw the face of Moses. That the skin of Moses' face shone: and Moses put the vail upon his face again, until he went in to speak with him.

So this was just an effect that the Word itself had upon Moses, and this was supposed to happen, for Moses regular skin represented the literal sense of the Word which Moses had been given from YHWH to give to the people upon the two tables of testimony, but by the face of Moses being shoned or glowing it represented the spiritual sense of the Word shining through from Divine wisdom which is the Word itself which is called as we know Yeshua and" in the beginning was the Word and the Word was with YHWH and the Word was YHWH".

The Word was with Moses and all the prophets in the same manner. For it was the same Spirit, but with unique differences in their signification as to the spiritual sense of the Word, which was represented by the literal words that they spoke as well as by the miraculous manifestations in their life.

However, Yeshua, because He was the Word itself, his whole face and body did not just shine. For the Word transfigure means to actually change form as to His face and body, whereby taking a different form he could represent that He was the Divine Word itself. Moses and Elijah remained in the form of men as to their spiritual bodys, for after

Yeshua was changed, then they appeared talking with Him. This was because He was the Divine Word itself shining as the Sun upon them. Demonstrating that not only was the Word from him, but that He was the word itself. This is a big difference my friend from any prophet, king, judge or ruler that ever existed in Israel. It never did nor could happen with any of them.

Besides, Yeshua Himself said:

John 15: 23 He that hateth me hateth my Father also.

24 IF I HAD NOT DONE AMONG THEM THE WORKS WHICH NONE OTHER MAN DID, THEY HAD NOT HAD SIN: but now have they both seen and hated both me and my Father.

25 But this cometh to pass, that the word might be fulfilled that is written in their law, they hated me without a cause.

26 But when the Comforter is come, whom I will send unto you from the Father, even the Spirit of truth, which proceedeth from the Father, he shall testify of me:

27 And ye also shall bear witness, because ye have been with me from the beginning."

It says here that He Himself will send the Spirit of Truth to them and we know this was fulfilled in Acts 2 in the upper room where it says:

2 And suddenly there came a sound from heaven as of a rushing mighty wind, and it filled the house where they were sitting.

4 And they were all filled with the Holy Ghost, and began to speak with other tongues, as the Spirit gave them utterance.

He also says that the Spirit shall TESTIFY of him and that they also would be witnesses. Notice he makes distinction between the Spirit and man's testimony. The Spirit's testimony is one and man's is another. Consequently the Spirit comes to us by way of enlightenment concerning who Yeshua is. Yeshua is the Word. The Spirit gives enlightenment from the Word. This is why Yeshua says He will send the Spirit to them from the Father. Let's think about this. How could He send the Spirit from the Father unless He Was the Father operating as the Son for the sake of mans redemption? Thereafter, sending his Spirit to all those that receive him, and thereby giving them power to become sons of the Living YHWH @Bob. This is the reason why the nature of his birth is important to understand. For by this we can understand that Yeshua is YHWH who has come in the flesh. Not by the seed of man, but by the Sprit of YHWH moving upon the egg of Mary to form a human body for himself in order that he may be born a man (called the Son) with like passions as we, but over coming them all by his Divine (called the Father) from within.

13

The spiritual and the natural world are two distinct realms

(That Elijah was taken up into heaven by the spirit and that his supernatural abilities were by the spirit)

To John: Have you not read of Elijah, who was taken, for as it is written *2 kings 2:*
9¶And it came to pass, when they were gone over, that Elijah said unto Elisha, Ask what I shall do for thee, before I be taken away from thee. And Elisha said, I pray thee, let a double portion of thy spirit be upon me.
10And he said, Thou hast asked a hard thing: nevertheless, if thou see me when I am taken from thee, it shall be so unto thee; but if not, it shall not be so.
11And it came to pass, as they still went on, and talked, that, behold, there appeared a chariot of fire, and horses of fire, and parted them both asunder; and Elijah went up by a whirlwind into heaven.
12¶ And Elisha saw it, and he cried my father, my father, the chariot of Israel, and the horsemen thereof. And he saw him no more: and he took hold of his own clothes, and rent them in two pieces.
13He took up also the mantle of Elijah that fell from him, and went back, and stood by the bank of Jordan;

14And he took the mantle of Elijah that fell from him, and smote the waters, and said, where is the Lord God of Elijah? And when he also had smitten the waters, they parted hither and thither: and Elisha went over.
15And when the sons of the prophets which were to view at Jericho saw him, they said, The spirit of Elijah doth rest on Elisha. And they came to meet him, and bowed themselves to the ground before him.

And there are others, but to the point. It is never heaven alone, but thy will be done on the earth as it is in heaven. The problem comes when you leave out one for the other, such as the Jews did. What good is the so called hypothalamus gland which is physical, without life which is spiritual activating it? What speech do you have without thought? What action without will. Come my friend surely you understand that YHWH who is spirit who created what was physical, and that the physical did not always exist like the Spirit did. Did not Elijah do what he did by the Spirit? My friend understand just as the head is formed first in the womb so the spirit is the first by which man has life in the body, for although Adam was created he did not become a living soul until YHWH breathed life into his nostrils. However, the quality of one's spiritual life determines his natural life, for this is the real person. With the mind you love or hate, the body only responds to the will of the mind. It is only a tool on earth nothing more. It does not determine who you really are. For the evil can do good works just like the righteous. But they cannot from evil bring forth good into the heart. Eternal life means a quality of life my brother not as to the body. That quality is essentially love, joy and peace and because these are attributes of the Holy Spirit they are therefore called Eternal, and because these are of the life of the Spirit they are called Life. The Love, Joy and Peace of the Spirit are not depended on earthly matters, but are become the very essence and make up one's soul.

14

The meaning of Israel being in Egypt for 400 yrs

To John: You must be careful to understand that the Word is written in a style unlike any that exist today. It is written in a certain way so that spiritual things as well as literal things can be understood. Like as you mentioned what was written in *"Gen 15:*
13 And he said unto Abram, Know of a surety that thy seed shall be a stranger in a land that is not theirs, and shall serve them; and they shall afflict them four hundred years;

14 And also that nation, whom they shall serve, will I judge: and afterward shall they come out with great substance.
But yet in *Exodus 12* we read:
40 Now the sojourning of the children of Israel, who dwelt in Egypt, was four hundred and thirty years.
41 And it came to pass at the end of the four hundred and thirty years, even the selfsame day it came to pass, that all the hosts of the Lord went out from the land of Egypt.
42 It is a night to be much observed unto the Lord for bringing them out from the land of Egypt: this is that night of the Lord to be observed of all the children of Israel in their generations.

So this tells you plainly how long they were there due to what I explained earlier. Please understand why the scriptures are pointing out 400 as to what was told Abraham or 430 which is according to the time that Abraham sojourned there. Because of what 4, 40, 400 represents. Spiritually it was used to denote affliction, however long or short the duration maybe which was 430 years, but as you pointed out the affliction itself was only 230 years, but again it is stating 430 for the reason that it involves 400 which again corresponds to trials and afflictions. This is way in Gen 15:13 it directly says 400 years instead of 430 years, which was the actual time. This is shown throughout the whole

Bible for example: As by 40 days and 40 nights of rain with Noah.

Ez 29:10 Behold, therefore I am against thee, and against thy rivers, and I will make the land of Egypt utterly waste and desolate, from the tower of Syene even unto the border of Ethiopia.

11No foot of man shall pass through it, nor foot of beast shall pass through it, neither shall it be inhabited forty years.

12And I will make the land of Egypt desolate in the midst of the countries that are desolate, and her cities among the cities that are laid waste shall be desolate forty years: and I will scatter the Egyptians among the nations, and will disperse them through the countries.

Rev 13:5 and there was given unto him a mouth speaking great things and blasphemies; and power was given unto him to continue forty and two months.

Rev 11:2 But the court which is without the temple leave out, and measure it not; for it is given unto the Gentiles: and the holy city shall they tread under foot forty and two months.

Israel wandered 40 years in the wilderness; Moses was 40 days and nights on Mt Sinai. Elijah 40 days and nights without eating, Yeshua himself fasted 40 days and nights. There are too much to put own. Likewise all the numbers of the Word were of great importance, because of great significance

15

Prophecy of Gen 15:14-16 is it referring to Israelites? Or black Americans?

To James: Sometimes to know what is prophetic you have to wait until it comes to pass. Until then I guess we will be debating. Lol

Anyway, YHWH did tell them to remember their deliverance from Egypt to all generations also He told them they would leave out with great substance and poses that land called Canaan which they did for these were Abraham's seed. Why would he not prophecy concerning these people who were to receive the Law and become a great nation. Again there is more to those scriptures for it is written: *Gen 15:*

14And also that nation, whom they shall serve, will I judge: and afterward shall they come out with great substance.

15 And thou shalt go to thy fathers in peace; thou shalt be buried in a good old age.

16 But in the fourth generation they shall come hither again: for the iniquity of the Amorites is not yet full.

Notice the last verse referring to the the 4th generation. Who else but these Israelites could this

be referring to, for no black slaves knew what an Amorite was. As I understand, it was more than 4 generations that passed by the time this happened. Again the 4th generation is an expression that occurs likewise in other places that only signifies ones restoration, because it is referring to the end of what is meant by 40 or 400 years.
And as you know Canaan was called the land of the Amorites.

Amos 2:9 Yet destroyed I the Amorite before them, whose height was like the height of the cedars, and he was strong as the oaks; yet I destroyed his fruit from above, and his roots from beneath.
10 Also I brought you up from the land of Egypt, and led you forty years through the wilderness, to possess the land of the Amorite.

Therefore Amorite in this passage is referring to the nations who were in the land of Canaan which Joshua and Israel had to fight. This could not in any way be referring to American slaves, but I understand the analogy. Analogies like this can be made throughout the whole bible in reference to many things. That is why the Scriptures are so great, because it can relate to all of humanities experience.

There is nothing in the Word without a spiritual meaning

Notes: All numbers as well as words in the Bible have a spiritual meaning. This should not be mysterious today. Numbers such as 3,7,12 are known to have a spiritual meaning seeing how they are used in the Word. But many or most in the church do not realize that all the numbers of the Bible have a spiritual meaning as well as all the words of the Bible. So how numbers are used in the Word is very significant to understanding the spiritual meaning to which the words of the Bible corresponds to. It must be understood, that before the Word became flesh it was spiritual. And since the Word is made up of truths, therefore the Word was made up of spiritual truths before it became literal or natural. These spiritual truths are what dwell in heaven among angels and it was thereafter given to men in the world. And since this world exists according to natural laws and order, the Word was therefore written in accordance with this in a natural language whereby men could have an understanding of the Word according to the intellect that they are born with. Notwithstanding the spiritual sense of the Word lies hidden in the natural sense. It is from this that the number 3, 7, 12 and so forth get their spiritual meaning. An example of this would be were light is mentioned in the Word it spiritually means truth and were darkness is mentioned it means falsities and this in accordance to the nature of the light or darkness the scripture is describing.

16
The meaning of Jesus saying that Abraham saw his day

To Brian: Well I'm just saying you art to consider how that Abraham saw His day and was glad. *In John 8:56 it says*
"Your father Abraham rejoiced to see my day: and he saw it, and was glad". Now if Abraham saw Yeshua that means He must be YHWH right? I mean if He really saw Yeshua with his eyes. Then there could be no doubt that He was YHWH for who is Yeshua that Abraham would rejoice to see His day. For it says *John 8:56*
Your father Abraham rejoiced to see my day: and he saw it, and was glad.
57 Then said the Jews unto him, Thou art not yet fifty years old, and hast thou seen Abraham?
58 Jesus said unto them, Verily, verily, I say unto you, Before Abraham was, I am.

So if this is true would not He of necessity have to be YHWH? For it is said in Gen 18:1 that the Lord appeared unto Abraham.

Numbers in the Bible

Note*: That all the numbers in the Word, especially the number seven has a spiritual meaning and not just a natural one is seen in many passages* *throughout the Bible. Anyone can see that seven is a number like any other number used in this world, but in the Word the number seven is used to denote something more than just a number. It is said on the seventh day God rested, but Apostle Paul explains that this means that we too enter into his rest by ceasing from our own works and that this is the meaning of entering into the Sabbath which is the seventh day. As he says in Hebrew 4:10*

10 For he that is entered into his rest, he also hath ceased from his own works, as God did from his. There are many other passages that use the number 7 with a significant meaning and not just as a number, such as Joshua 6:

4 And seven priests shall bear before the ark seven trumpets of rams' horns: and the seventh day ye shall compass the city seven times, and the priests shall blow with the trumpets.

Why would God want to use 7 priests with seven trumpets, to walk around the city seven times if the number seven did not have a significant use among them? There is purpose and meaning in all things that God does and says, for He is Purpose Divine and meaning Divine. Therefore, all things He does and says must have purpose and meaning in it, for these are of His essence. Without it, it would be vain to use the number seven and we all know that God is not vain, but He is full of purpose, meaning and use, besides He tells us in the Ten Commandments to not even use His name in vain and that He would not hold him guiltless who does so. And we all know a hypocrite is a fake person that tells people to do things that he doesn't do himself and surely we know God is no hypocrite for as it is written "Be ye holy for I am holy". Besides, Divine wisdom must have within it purpose (the goal or intended outcome of something), meaning (what something signifies or indicates) and use (to put something into action or service for some purpose), without which, it would be vain or empty not having the things of which wisdom consist. All this is said that it might be understood that God does not do anything for any reason at anytime the way He wants to like as men are want to do, but He himself does all things by the Divine order which is according to the nature of His Divine essence, which are Divine love and wisdom and there can be no wisdom without purpose and meaning, so there can be no purpose and meaning without wisdom.

17
YHWH appearing in human form to Abraham

To James: YHWH appeared to Abraham and Yeshua said He rejoiced to see my day. How do you think YHWH appeared to Abraham when He is present everywhere. He had to have used a human form and that human form of God was called Yeshua (Jesus) for how else could he say *"Abraham rejoiced to see my day"* or say *"before Abraham was I AM"*. He also said in *Luke10:*

18 And he said unto them, I beheld Satan as lightning fall from heaven.

Now how could this be when this was before all mankind? Surely Yeshua is not a liar and a fake or just making thinks up. For whenever he spoke in parables He would tell his disciples about it for he said it is given for them to know the mysteries of the kingdom.

Three essentials that make one God

Notes: Just as H2O has three different states, which are water (a liquid state), ice (a solid state) and vapor (a gaseous state), yet all three different states are in essence one element which is H2O. So

also does God exist as to three different states of the Divine, these are the Divine itself (the Father), the Divine human (the Son) and the Divine proceeding (the Holy Spirit), yet all three states are of one Divine which is God himself. For God this would be easy, due to the fact that He is present everywhere at one time. This is why the Lord said to his disciples "Lo I am with you always even unto the end of the world" For He would be present everywhere with them as God in the image of the Son. Again, this is why the Lord said "All power is given unto me in heaven and in earth" For God had given his human all power and authority over all humanity, for this human was his body born from Mary and was named Jesus Christ the Savior of the world and called the Son of God. He is called the Son, because he allowed himself to be born the same way any child is born and is given the title son or daughter, but because his body was produced by God himself he was called the Son of God. And because no one had true access to the God except by his human, Jesus, the name given to the humanity of God in the flesh, therefore said unto them in John 14:6 "no man cometh unto the Father, but by me." Also He says in John 1:18
No man hath seen God at any time; the only begotten Son, which is in the bosom of the Father, he hath declared him.

The term begotten means to be a direct descendant. This is why he said he is in the bosom of the Father, meaning he came forth from the Father. Just as a son is in the bosom or loins of their father at the time the seed is produced, and from there comes forth. This is why he said unto the Jews in John 8:42

"42 Jesus said unto them, If God were your Father, ye would love me: for I proceeded forth and came from God; neither came I of myself, but he sent me." This is referring to the divine nature of his birth, which is that his body was produced inside of Mary by the Divine proceeding from the Divine itself. And that the body could not and did not come forth of itself is meant by the Lord saying "neither came I of myself, but he sent me."

That "he hath declared him" means to reveal him or to make him known. This is why he told Thomas in John 14:

"7 If ye had known me, ye should have known my Father also: and from henceforth ye know him, and have seen him." And to Philip he says:

"9 Jesus saith unto him, Have I been so long time with you, and yet hast thou not known me, Philip? he that hath seen me hath seen the Father; and how sayest thou then, Shew us the Father?

10 Believest thou not that I am in the Father, and the Father in me? the words that I speak unto you I speak not of myself: but the Father that dwelleth in me, he doeth the works."

It should be understood that the body does nothing of itself without its spirit. That is why the Lord says in John 6:63 "It is the spirit that quickeneth; the flesh profiteth nothing:" That the spirit in him is what was called the Father and that the flesh is what was called the Son can be seen in the fact the Lord says "the Father that dwellth in me, he doeth the works." The spirit and body acting as one is what is meant by the Father and the Son are one.

18
YHWH appearing in human form to Abraham (Continuation)

To Brian: When YHWH appeared unto Abraham in the flesh, (Gen 18:1) it was during the time that He was told Sarah would conceive. This was not a vision. Also in

Gen 17:

1 And when Abram was ninety years old and nine, the Lord appeared to Abram, and said unto him, I am the Almighty God; walk before me, and be thou perfect.

2 And I will make my covenant between me and thee, and will multiply thee exceedingly.

3 And Abram fell on his face: and God talked with him, saying,

4 As for me, behold, my covenant is with thee, and thou shalt be a father of many nations.
5 Neither shall thy name any more be called Abram, but thy name shall be Abraham; for a father of many nations have I made thee.
John 8:56
Your father Abraham rejoiced to see my day: and he saw it, and was glad.
57 Then said the Jews unto him, Thou art not yet fifty years old, and hast thou seen Abraham?
58 Jesus said unto them, Verily, verily, I say unto you, before Abraham was, I am.

There is just simply no mistake about what Yeshua is saying. It is so plain even I hate to add to it. Who else would appear to Abraham as YHWH? Why would YHWH not appear to us as Savior when besides him there is no other Savior? It's plain that Yeshua is YHWH in the flesh.

The Bible says One God, but man says Three Gods

Notes: *According to the Athanasian Creed the Father, the Son and Holy Spirit are all completely separate individuals that abide as one. That is they coexist as one. For as it reads:*
"3. And the catholic faith is this: That we worship one God in Trinity, and Trinity in Unity;
4. Neither confounding the persons nor dividing the substance.

5. For there is one person of the Father, another of the Son, and another of the Holy Spirit.
6. But the Godhead of the Father, of the Son, and of the Holy Spirit is all one, the glory equal, the majesty coeternal."

So if you do not confound the persons, it means they are separate individuals, nor dividing the substance would mean they all partake of the same essence which would make them equally God as much as the other. Consequently, if this is true, how could it be that when you see the Son you see the Father, when the Son is a different person from eternity than the Father? And if the Son came from eternity and clothed himself with a body, then it is in truth not the Father himself in person who clothed himself with a body. For although, each one is said to be God and to be one, it still says "Neither confounding the persons", which means they are separate individuals and although one can represent the other, yet they are not the other, for they are all distinct persons, which means the Son cannot be the Father nor the Father the Son, for they are not the same person neither can they represent each other as the same person for they are different individuals. This therefore totally contradicts what is said in Isaiah 9:6
"For unto us a child is born, unto us a son is given: and the government shall be upon his shoulder: and his name shall be called Wonderful, Counsellor, The mighty God, <u>The everlasting</u>

Father, The Prince of Peace." (For how can the Son be called The everlasting Father, when there is only one Father which is God in heaven) If so be that the Athanasian Creed is correct in saying that "there is one person of the Father, another of the Son, and another of the Holy Spirit." Let us all be mindful to use the scriptures to test if Creeds are correct and not use Creeds to test if the Scriptures are correct, despite who may have written them. For the scriptures are directly from Gods mouth and not from any private interpretations as confirmed in
2 Peter 1:20
20 Knowing this first, that no prophecy of the scripture is of any private interpretation.

19
YHWH appearing in human form to Abraham (Continuation)

To James: Reincarnation is when a person dies and then is reborn in another body. This could not apply to Yeshua seeing he was not born yet. So YHWH appearing to Abraham in the flesh would make this to be incarnation. Consequently YHWH without flesh is YHWH but YHWH incarnated is Yeshua not as another person, but as the express image of his person.

The Fullness of the Godhead is in Christ Jesus bodily

Notes*: This is why the Lord Jesus said Abraham rejoiced to see his day and that he saw it and was glad. How else could Abraham have seen Jesus if he did not appear to him in human form? For outside of the human form no one, according to the scriptures can behold Gods face and live. This is what was told Moses in Ex 33:20*

"And he said, Thou canst not see my face: for there shall no man see me, and live." And yet it in the book of Deuteronomy it says He knew Moses face to face, Duet 34:10

"And there arose not a prophet since in Israel like unto Moses, whom the Lord knew face to face". And yet He still appeared unto Abraham, Isaac and Jacob the patriarchs of Israel. It should be understood that God is present everywhere at one time, so therefore man cannot see God as he is in himself, because man cannot see everywhere at one time. This is what is meant when the scriptures says "No man can see the face of God and live, for to see the Face of God would be to see him everywhere at one time not just in the world, but throughout space. For man this is not possible, because his life as well as angels is finite or limited, but with God this is possible, because his life is infinite or unlimited. It being told Moses and all others that man cannot see Gods face and live,

signifies that man cannot see God everywhere at the same time and remain alive, for this would not be mans life, but Gods life as to his Divine itself, for this is unlimited. This is why it is said in John 1:18

"No man hath seen God at any time; the only begotten Son, which is in the bosom of the Father, he hath declared him." That is revealed him. However, because man is finite, he is able to see within the scope of his vision an express image of God, for this is in a finite form, which according to scripture is the human form as to the appearance of a man. In this way man can see Gods face and live. This is why the scriptures turns around and says that God knew Moses face to face, when before it was said no man can see his face and live. It was said in Duet 34:10 "And there arose not a prophet since in Israel like unto Moses, whom the Lord knew face to face". The reason why Moses is singled out is because by Moses is signified the Divine truth and to see Gods face as one representing Divine truth is greater than seeing Gods face as one who represents the doctrine which is from Divine truth, which is what all the other prophets represented, for by Moses the Law of the covenant or Old Testament was established, but by the prophets this was to be maintained and as much as possible enforced until the Lord himself came. And that He also appeared to the prophets as a man, is also mentioned in Ez 1:26

26 And above the firmament that was over their heads was the likeness of a throne, as the appearance of a sapphire stone: and upon the likeness of the throne was the likeness as the appearance of a man above upon it."
So God appeared to them as a man in a human form and this human form is what is called the Lord Jesus Christ, which is the express image of God, according to what Paul says in Hebrew 1:3"Who being the brightness of his glory, and the <u>express image of his person,</u>." This is why the Lord said in John 8:56

"Your father Abraham rejoiced to see my day: and he saw it, and was glad."
Although, they at that time did not know him by the name Jesus Christ, He was yet and still acknowledged as the Lord God. So in our time the human body of God as we know it is called the Lord Jesus Christ. Without the human form he cannot be seen, for he is everywhere present at one time as to his Divine itself, which is omnipresent, by which He was able to create and bring forth all things everywhere throughout the universe, even his Son, which is why outside of the body He is called the Father, who is unlimited. In the body He is called the Son, who was limited, but after his resurrection his body was glorified and became one and the selfsame substance as the Divine itself, whereby it is said in Matt 28:18

"And Jesus came and spake unto them, saying, All power is given unto me in heaven and in earth." And that he also said *"Lo I am with you always even unto the end of the world".* When previously before his resurrection or glorification He said to them in Matt 26: 11 *"For ye have the poor always with you; but me ye have not always."* Again, his body before his glorification was limited. This why He said

John 14:28

"Ye have heard how I said unto you, I go away, and come again unto you. If ye loved me, ye would rejoice, because I said, I go unto the Father: for my Father is greater than I." Again, outside the body He is called the Father, as to which he is unlimited, but within the body, before his glorification He is called the Son, which was limited, therefore He said *"I go unto the Father"* which means that by the glorification of his body He would become one with the Divine itself called the Father, after which he came back to them saying *"all power is given unto me"* for now the Father and the Son had became one and the same. This is why He prayed to what was called the Father like any other man, for the state of God in the body as to his birth, which was like any other man is different from his state outside the body which is not like any man, but it is without bounds, this why the Lord prayed like any other man to the Father, and this is how he conquered all sin in the

body unlike any other man, for unlike any other man he was born from the Divine itself and not by any seed produced by man. By this, one can understand the relationship and events concerning the Father and the Son written in the gospels.

20

Spiritual love brought by the Divine human

To James: My joy is fulfilled when I love others the way He showed us all how to love for it is written: by this love shall all men know ye are my disciples. Not by me loving only them who do well to me, but by me loving them who hate, despise, or just misunderstand me. In this way I can love the way he loved and forgive the way he forgave. For he is my peace as he says: *My peace I give unto you not as the world giveth, but give I unto you.* And this is the bread I have eaten and now I have eternal life in me and will live forever, for this love is forever, for it is above all and being from eternity it is before all. To live forever is not a matter of time, but without time. Time is put off and eternity is put on, but for now while I am in time I have eternal life abiding in me. There is power in knowing who Yeshua is, because the love

peace and joy you have through him is from above for as he said *"I am from above ye are from beneath"*. Consequently it is Divine and not earthly. So as he forgives me reproves me and chastens me in spirit. I feel more enabled in sprit to forgive others and to do for others and as I look to him I sense more of him in me and no more I. It is not so much the doing for others and forgiving of others that you are empowered with, but the quality of the state of mind in which you do it for this is your spirit where YHWH dwells as in his temple. So now we have YHWH
showing his love through Yeshua and Yeshua showing his love through us unto the world.

The essence of one's love defines the nature of their life

Notes: Just as the heart is said to be the center of the body so love is the center of who a person is. The heart denotes what is most important. So when we say "do this" or "do that from the heart", it means to do it in or from love. And when we do it from love, it is then that we are doing the best that we can. It said the greatest commandment is to love the Lord thy God with all your heart. We all know that the physical heart of the body cannot love or feel emotions like sadness or joy. The mind does that. The heart just pumps blood continually throughout the body and it does this by receiving impulses through nerve fibers connected to it from the brain. So that this happens wither we want it to or not, wither we are sleep or awake, thinking or not thinking, and this because it is mechanical and automatic. The reason why it is said to love the Lord thy God with all your heart is because the heart is the symbol of all the affection and love of a man's life. It is said that the "life is in the blood", but furthermore the blood is from the heart. So the blood is continually being sent out by the heart to all parts of the body for its renewing and constant nourishment. Therefore, if the heart or love is the center of a person's life, it must also be the essential thing that determines the quality of a person's life. When we say "he has an evil heart" we essentially mean he is an evil person or "he has a good heart "we essentially mean he is a good person. It is the quality of our love that determines wither we essentially are good or evil at heart. The love of money is said to be evil, because anybody who willfully gives them money, they love, but those who hold it back despite any good reason, they despise, for the love of money is their principal love. The "love of self" as it is called is also said to be evil, because when a person is in the love of themselves, they love only those who favor their ideas, wants and desires and anyone feeling indifferent they despise, even if the person has good intentions in doing so, for the love of self is their principal love. To love thy neighbor as thyself is said to be good, because in this one values the life of another as much as himself. Through this way they live in harmony with one another, despite their differences of opinion, for it is the life that is valued and loved. This is because loving their neighbor as themselves is their principal love. This love is from the Lord and is unconditional, for it is spiritual; all other loves not from the Lord are conditional, for they are concerning self and the world. So when a person is sent to jail for their wrong doing, it does not appear to be love, but the hope is that they will learn not to do evil to others or to themselves and this in the end is love, for in gaining this, he learns to value the life of others as well as his own ,but again apart from the Lord this love is only natural and not spiritual, for he then only values the life of others due to fear of retaliation by others, penalties of the law, loss of reputation and the like that are merely based on natural loses.

21

Christ is represented by the Kings of Israel

To James: All the kings good and bad represented the Lord as ruler over Israel, especially David for He was a Prophet and often when He spoke of himself it was concerning the Lord. For as I believe the Lord is the Word. There is nothing there that does not bear reference to Him and his kingdom in one way or the other for it is his Divinity that makes the Word Holy. Now whether they were bad or good that was on them, but as King, there is only one true eternal one and they represented Him who was and is and forever will be King.

The Doctrine of representations in the OT

Notes: It is said that all the kings of Israel represented the Lord who is King of Kings. This is because Israel as well as all the things written in the Old Testament represented the Lord and the Christian Kingdom established in the New Testament. As for instance all the judges and all the kings and all the prophets and even the priests as well as all the leaders of Israel represented the Lord himself among his people as to the work of their salvation. This is why it was imperative that they obeyed the Law of Moses and the word of the prophets, unlike today whereas the Law of Moses and the Word of the prophets is the Word of God revealed unto us in Christ Jesus. They, not having Christ at that

time, were given substitutes that stood in his place until he should come, such as the judges, the kings, the prophets and the priests. These, together with all the Laws and commandments as well as the people who were to obey them (Israel) represented the Lord Himself and his kingdom on earth, which came to pass after he was born in the world. Why else would it have been taken so seriously that they should obey the laws, such as not doing any labor on the Sabbath day or else if they did they would be put to death? If there were not in these Laws spiritual things that pertained to something more holy and divine among them, other than the sense of the letter of the Law. It should be understood that just as there is a spiritual body and a natural body so also there are spiritual laws and natural laws. The two are not the same. In this life the one corresponds to the other, so that the Laws that were given to them, although literally they pertained to their natural living, they came forth from spiritual laws that pertain to spiritual living, for God who first is a spirit spoke and brought them forth into the natural which was. And because it was God who spoke and brought forth the Law of Moses and the word of the prophets into the natural, it posses power, for the life of the Word which includes His commandments are directly from Him and by him whereby if they are obeyed they cannot fail. Therefore, as was said it was imperative that they did and said according to all that the Lord had commanded them. For in it, that is in his Word which includes his commandments (thus the bible itself) there dwells within it the spiritual sense of the Word due to the presence of God within it (being that in essence He is the Word and its very life). As long as they obeyed these commandments it symbolized that they spiritually obeyed him and were consequently blessed throughout their life. Again, it only represented that they spiritually obeyed him, not that they did, for they could not, because the Holy Spirit, by which one obeys God spiritually was not yet given. For, if they were spiritual they would not have needed the Law of Moses to represent spiritual laws in order for them to be connected to God. For, God is a spirit and to be connected to God "they that worship him must worship him in spirit and in truth" Jn 4:24. Therefore it was given them that by obeying the Law of Moses which pertained to worship by animal sacrifices and offerings and other worldly laws, it thereby symbolized obedience to spiritual laws, which pertained to spiritual life. This is why he brought forth the Law, that by a law corresponding to spiritual laws He could thereby be among them and bless them correspondingly through the Law. Who cannot see that this is why they were so blessed throughout their land above all nations and could destroy all their enemies who were greater than themselves and that He kept all sickness and disease from among them so long as they obeyed the Law that was given them. And how they were cursed above all nations and could not destroy their enemies, but would become their captives, and would come into all manner of sickness and diseases so long as they did not obey the Laws that were given them. And this even until Christ came and took away the representative blessings that came by way of the Law and established the true spiritual blessings that come by way of grace and truth. For in Christ we are become spiritual, for He is greater than the law, in that He brought forth a greater Testament in his blood, for all things of the law represented spiritual and heavenly things that are in Him, which he has now brought to us by way of His Holy Spirit.

22

The difference between spiritual gifts and spiritual faculties of the mind

To Brian: Spiritual faculties and Spiritual Gifts are two different things. Spiritual faculties or faculties of the spirit are what enable us to have thought concepts. These faculties are what are called rationality by which we reason, memory by which we store knowledge of various kinds and reflect on them and use them to confirm truths that we learn. There are more, but the point is that gentiles can use them to understand spiritual matters (what you call Torah) as well as Jews. All men are born with this. Without it a man would not be able to reflect, think, or reason. Thus without it man would not be man. The spiritual that I am speaking of is simply referring to what is intangible, nonphysical and immaterial in regard to the spoken of faculties of the mind by which we reflect, think and reason, thus by which we are human.

However, the spiritual that Paul speaks of is regarding a quality of life that we receive by the Holy Spirit. This is achieved by the complete submission of all the faculties of the mind surrendered unto the Lord. He in return endows us with all spiritual good and truth. From this they

receive a new essence of life, which is identified as being born again. As Yeshua say's
Jn 3:
6 That which is born of the flesh is flesh; and that which is born of the Spirit is spirit.
7 Marvel not that I said unto thee, ye must be born again.
8 The wind bloweth where it listeth, and thou hearest the sound thereof, but canst not tell whence it cometh, and whither it goeth: so is every one that is born of the Spirit.
He that is born of the Spirit comes into spiritual gifts or abilities by which he is enabled to perceive and do supernatural things without ever having to know them or be able to perform them themselves. They that are born of the Spirit are they who Paul says in:
1 cor 12:
and that no man can say that Jesus is the Lord, but by the Holy Spirit.
Everyone by birth is born with spiritual faculties. By these spiritual faculties anyone can say Jesus is Lord or Jesus is not Lord. They can curse Jesus and they can bless him too. So therefore Paul cannot be referring to this.
What Paul is referring to is a quality of life that one comes into by the Holy Spirit. This quality of life or inspiration which comes only from above is the Spirit by which one confesses from the heart that Jesus is Lord. It is the same Spirit by which

we cry Abba. It is the same spirit Yeshua spoke of
to his disciples and said in
Acts 1:8
But ye shall receive power, after that the Holy
Spirit is come upon you: and ye shall be witnesses
unto me both in Jerusalem, and in all Judœa, and
in Samaria, and unto the uttermost part of the
earth. It is the same Spirit by which Paul when he
had laid hands on them:
Acts 19:
6 And when Paul had laid his hands upon them,
the Holy Spirit came on them; and they spake with
tongues, and prophesied.
It is the same Spirit by which these spiritual gifts
are distributed in 1 cor 1

23

Spiritual gifts refer to supernatural power not natural professions/talents

To James: It is said that the spirit gives the
interpretation. My friend your understanding of
spiritual things are actually not spiritual, but
natural. Even the definitions you have are all
understood naturally, not spiritually. In verse 1 the
Authorized Version (KJV) mentions "spiritual
gifts." The Greek simply reads "spirituals" (ton
pneumatikon), meaning "things characterized or
controlled by the Spirit." Spiritual gifts, then, are
first of all things controlled or characterized by the

Spirit and not controlled or characterized by earthly or worldly knowlegde.

<u>Healing</u>" iaomai"simply is cure or (the effect)
<u>Miracle</u>"dunamis"simply is force, power
<u>Prophecy</u>"propheteia" simply is prediction
<u>Faith</u>"Pistis" simply is faithfulness, belief, believe
<u>Tongue</u>"glossa"simply is language (Specifically one not naturally acquired)

You choose to take it to mean it in a natural understanding and not a supernatural. You're completely out of context with all three chapters that deal with this subject. Think about it. Why would Paul say *"though I speak with the tongues of men and angels and though I have faith to move mountains"*? It is the same Faith "Pistis" in 1 corth 12.

This is not spiritual, but natural understanding you are talking about. The spirit did not and does not give knowledge to be healed by medicine you go to school for that. However, if he does give this knowledge by way of a spiritual gift, it would be revealed to the believer by what is called "the word of knowledge" in 1 corth 12:8 and not by any earthly education. It does not give you a degree to be a pharmacist, again you go to school for that. *"But the manifestation of the Spirit is given to every man to profit withal"*.

Understand that what you are explaining are not manifestations of the Spirit, but an understanding that comes by way of being educated in school.

This has nothing to do with the Spirit. I think you're a little mixed up, because you said "if you pray for YHWH to heal you and he doesn't". Don't you see that praying for God to heal you by His spirit is different from being healed by medicine? When you pray or ask YHWH for healing or a "cure" or "to be made whole" this can happen by way of the natural or by way of the Spirit which was done many times throughout the Bible supernaturally. These definitions mean nothing. Everyone who is healed is healed by one way or the other (all miracles happen by power or force whether it be divine miracles or earthly labor) the word healing is still the same it doesn't change the fact that one is either healed by the Spirit or by medicine (it is still a cure). It is the way that one is healed that determines that. The word GIFT here means "spiritual endowment' spiritual my friend not natural. That means they were given that ability by the Holy Spirit which abides within. Not by going to school to be a doctor. Paul worked miracles by the gift of the Holy Spirit so this means this was a spiritual gift that he possessed. Please understand also that your context of these scriptures are totally out of line with all of the NT context of healing and of miracles and of tongues and of faith, perhaps this will help you to understand how to look at these chapters 12,13,and 14 of 1 Corinthians.

24

God who is Spirit confounds the language of Babel by the Spirit

To James: *Gen 11*

6 And the Lord said, Behold, the people is one, and they have all one language; and this they begin to do: and now nothing will be restrained from them, which they have imagined to do.

7 Go to, let us go down, and there confound their language, that they may not understand one another's speech.

8 So the Lord scattered them abroad from thence upon the face of all the earth: and they left off to build the city.

9 Therefore is the name of it called Babel; because the Lord did there confound the language of all the earth: and from thence did the Lord scatter them abroad upon the face of all the earth.

To Carl, will you change what this means too. It says YHWH himself confounded their language. Isn't YHWH a Spirit? Did he (the Spirit) not cause them to speak in other tongues to each other? Wouldn't you say this was done in a supernatural way by the Spirit?

Why is it hard for you to accept that 1 Cor 12 is dealing with supernatural abilities that come by way of the Spirit? And because they come by way of the Spirit they are called spiritual gifts.

Man is born with spiritual faculties by which he thinks, reflects, and reason. Until he matures he uses these abilities to understand natural and civil and even moral laws, but when He matures he uses these spiritual faculties to understand spiritual truths (which has regard to the state of the mind and quality of the thoughts and affections to which they pertain) and a life according to them and not just natural things which has regard to our bodies and our life in this world among each other.
The word Spirit can mean the breath in your body as you say" breath/wind coming from our windpipe" or it can refer to as Mark says" Ruahk or Spirit also means intellect, thoughts concepts. But these are two distinct things that correspond to each other by which they make a one. The one refers to life (Ruahk-intellect, thought concept) as to ones spirit the other refers to life (Ruahk-breath/wind) in the body. The two meanings of Spirit consequently are referring to the two states of life one as to the soul the other as to the body. We are all born into these two states of life my friend without them there could be no life as to the soul or the body. So you see if spiritual faculties are what you are calling spiritual gifts then my friend the gentile has this as well as the Jews. The Atheist has this as well as the believer. The bond has this as well as the free. The devil has this as well as Angels.

So what is the matter? I gave you definitions as you gave me. For example:

<u>Prophecy</u> "propheteia" simply is prediction; reveal the secrets of men's hearts (1 Cor. 14:3, 23-25) as well as the rest.

<u>Healing</u>" iaomai" simply is cure or (the effect) Physical healing is a symbol of how God wants to heal all of us spiritually. An example: Peter and John's experience with the lame man at the temple gate (Acts 3:2-10).

<u>Miracle</u>"dunamis" simply is force, power. The spiritual ability to do works of a supernatural origin and character, such as could not be produced by natural agents and means. Philip (Acts 8:13), and Paul (Acts 13:9-12).

.

<u>Prophecy</u>"propheteia" simply is prediction.

<u>Faith</u>"Pistis" simply is faithfulness, belief, believe. The spiritual ability to see what isn't, believe it to be, and trust God to do it in His way and time, also faith to move mountains.

<u>Tongue</u>"glossa" simply is language (Specifically one not naturally acquired) the spiritual ability to speak an unknown foreign language without learning it beforehand.

<u>Interpretation</u>" hermeneis" The one who does the translation of that foreign tongue would be able, by the spirit, to interpret without learning the language beforehand (1 Cor. 14:27)

The way you choose to understand 1 Cor 12, 13, 14 does not change the fact that the entire NT speaks of these abilities as Spiritual gifts. That is supernatural abilities by way of the spirit.
They are the same exact words with the same Hebrew and Greek meanings. You are at liberty to view 1 Cor 12 the way you will, but Bro it is so far out of touch with what a miracle is throughout the whole bible that I think you really need to consider these points. Good luck. LOL

25

The meaning of the gift of tongues and prophecy

(This individual began to speak in an unknown tongue during his Jewish temple service. He said he didn't realize what was happening to him, all he knew was that he could not control what he was saying, but the Elders of the temple taught him that speaking in an unknown tongue is not from God, but from Satan)

To Brian: In 1 cor 13:1, this verse does not imply that he cannot speak in the tongues of angels it's just saying although he could speak it (have the ability) and have not love, it would not profit.
To John:

I agree with you on this point. But I would also like to reason with you. I applaud you for sharing your experience of speaking in an unknown tongue and would ask you to consider the fact that you were in worship when this happened. You were in a spiritual delight as to your heart. Now either your heart is occupied by Satan or by YHWH. It cannot be occupied by both. Could it be that you were filled with the Spirit of the Lord and you spoke things by the grace of YHWH so that it was no more you, but the Spirit of God operating through you? Consequently this had nothing to do with you at all, but the Spirit of God operating through you. Also as you mentioned tongues are for the edification of non-believers. But be careful for it does not say that it was to edify, but that it was for a sign to unbelievers that they were just that unbelievers and so by this miraculous sign not only would it represent that they were unbelievers, but it would indicate to them that there was something more that the Lord wanted to share with them as to becoming believers.

Therefore Paul wrote*"1 cor 14*

21 In the law it is written, with men of other tongues and other lips will I speak unto this people; and yet for all that will they not hear me, saith the Lord.

Therefore tongues are only a representative or sign of people who do not believe, "because they will not hear me or hearken to me Saith the Lord".

When you speak in tongues it doesn't mean you are anyone else around you are unbelievers. This is only telling you what that gift signifies or symbolizes. When you are operating in that gift it does not mean that there are unbelievers with you in the room at all. This is only an exegesis of that gift. So Paul goes on to say:

22 Wherefore tongues are for a sign, not to them that believe, but to them that believe not: but prophesying serveth not for them that believe not, but for them which believe.

Whereby if one Prophecy it is a sign that it is for believers, not that everyone is a believer it is just a sign by way to indicate that it is for believers due to the fact that they can hear and understand what is being said. However, it does not imply that they are actual believers of the faith. Notwithstanding, these signs follow those that believe. Again Paul's explanation is only an exegesis of these gifts. This is why for the sake of understanding he goes on to say:

1 cor 14

23 If therefore the whole church be come together into one place and all speak with tongues, and there come in those that are unlearned, or unbelievers, will they not say that ye are mad?

24 But if all prophesy, and there come in one that believeth not, or one unlearned, he is convinced of all, he is judged of all: (See the prophecy he says is

also for the unbeliever for the sake of understanding.)
25 And thus are the secrets of his heart made manifest; and so falling down on his face he will worship God, and report that God is in you of a truth.
For tongues he says again:
2 For he that speaketh in an unknown tongue speaketh not unto men, but unto God: for no man understandeth him; howbeit in the spirit he speaketh mysteries.
Thus for prophecy he says:
3 But he that prophesieth speaketh unto men to edification, and exhortation, and comfort. (That is to their understanding and comprehension unto the edifying of all). So with tongues he goes on to say:
14 For if I pray in an unknown tongue, my spirit prayeth, but my understanding is unfruitful.
15What is it then? I will pray with the spirit, and I will pray with the understanding also: I will sing with the spirit, and I will sing with the understanding also.

How can one speak in an unknown tongue and not know what it means? This could only be possible if the Spirit was operating through him and using him to say such things out of his mouth without him ever learning it. It is a miraculous gift of grace and has nothing to do with one's own natural abilities or what he has learned from others. This is why he says:

13 Wherefore let him that speaketh in an unknown tongue pray that he may interpret.

26
Explanation of the rise and fall of man

To James: To be honest with you the letter of the Word can be manipulated in many ways to confirm any ones dogmas, but if I may. Everything as to creation has a natural and a spiritual co-existence. I say this because YHWH is Spiritual and from this the natural was brought forth. Consequently without the spiritual there can be no natural. In the beginning the natural was in sync with the spiritual. YHWH is said to have talked with man, the earth was peaceful, and the animals were pleasant. Life was in its fullness and delight. Everything in the earth corresponded with everything spiritual in heaven. This is why the earth was pleasant. The main cause of this was mans conjunction with the Lord. Man was given dominion over the earth. So long as his spirit was in order with YHWH, so long the earth and his body would prosper and be in good health and production. A likeness of this was seen in Israel so long as they obeyed YHWH the earth would bring forth in abundance to them, but whenever sin was in the camp they would suffer famine and disease. So mans spirit had turned from YHWH to himself, and the way he saw things before was not ever seen again. And so the earth became corrupt, because mans spirit which previously was in line with YHWH's, became corrupt and this thereby corrupted his natural life. So now man cannot see things as he saw it when His spirit looked up to YHWH, but now he sees things in a carnal way, because his spirit looks down toward himself and the world.

Therefore, the Lord had to eventually come and save the world from a complete destruction. The Divine itself was the spirit of his body and because he was above all he overcame all and died without sin, thus starting a new dispensation for the human race for righteousness to reign again as well as for all others who would look to him. However he promised to return again, because mans spirit would still look down to himself and the world. Only this time it would be worse, because now the Word was being used in a corrupt manner. This same Word that was to make a difference all throughout humanity was now being desecrated to make themselves rulers and even gods in the earth, even justifying every shameful act in the name of religion by the Word of God. He, who therefore, looks to himself and the world, consequently cannot help but falsify the Word to favor the love of self and thereby brings himself into damnation. But he who looks up to YHWH with the life and love of heaven, views the word translucently from the divine wherein are nothing, but plain truths holy and pure, all of which favor love to the Lord and to the neighbor, which consequently brings them all into eternal life.

No natural universe without a spiritual universe

Notes: The Bible was written in a way that spiritual ideas can be present within the literal words that are read. Nothing is written in the bible without a spiritual meaning within it. This is because God is a spirit and since the Word is from God, it too is spirit, but the natural meaning of the Bible is brought forth by natural words that correspond to its spiritual meanings from whence they come. It is what these natural words corresponds to that are called spiritual, but in its natural outward appearance the Word looks like any other book. Nevertheless, the literal words themselves correspond to spiritual things from which they protrude. To explain this a little it would go like this: Man is born natural and is primarily at birth concerned with only natural things of life such as food, water and all the necessities a natural of life even his thinking is merely about this, whereas until he becomes spiritual his reasoning is merely about natural things and concepts of life, but when he becomes spiritual he then thinks concerning spiritual things of life such as spiritual food and water and all the necessities and concepts of a spiritual life and not just his natural life. However, God is first spiritual therefore all things He creates are from a spiritual perspective; consequently all things in creation are in an image and form corresponding to some spiritual concept and quality. It is as if God clothed spiritual concepts with natural substances in order for things to have existence on a natural level and this is how the natural universe came into existence. He just clothed Divine spiritual things that were always there with natural substances by which came the creation of the natural universe. This is like what Apostle Paul says Hebrews 11:3

"3 Through faith we understand that the worlds were framed by the word of God, so that things which are seen were not made of things which do appear."

It is also like God Himself who is a Spirit when He clothed himself with flesh and blood and became a man among us and called himself Jesus Christ our Lord and Savior. It is the same with the bible, for the words are spiritual in essence because they came from God who is a spirit and these spiritual concepts or meanings were clothed with natural concepts or meanings by which we have the literal words of the Bible itself. This is why all things that are written in the Bible have a spiritual meaning within it. The story of creation was written in accordance to this, meaning that it was written in correspondence to spiritual ideas and order. For the fact of the matter is that God did not need six days to create heaven and earth. It was written that way so that spiritual concepts, ideas and order maybe represented by natural concepts, ideas and order. This is true concerning all things written about creation, such as God forming woman out of the rib of Adam, the snake speaking to Eve in the garden. Or the tree of the knowledge of good and evil how that it was said at first to be on the outside of the garden and then later said to be in the midst of the garden. Or how it was said that in the beginning of creation God created light by saying "let there be light" and "that the evening and the morning were the first day", but later, it says that on the fourth day God created all the lights of the heavens such as the sun, moon and stars. Who cannot see that there is more to this than just creation?, for by the natural understanding of the literal words of the bible there is a correspondence to spiritual concepts, ideas and order being here within it set forth and described.

27

The Word understood naturally is different when understood spiritually

As it was written before in *"John 6:32 To John and All: "Then Jesus said unto them, Verily, verily, I say unto you, Moses gave you not that bread from heaven; but my Father giveth you the true bread from heaven"*

The bread He speaks of is not natural, but spiritual. (The manner does not even refer to food, but teachings, referring to ones natural life which is the manna Moses gave to the people of those times, but the manna from heaven are teachings referring to ones spiritual life which is the true bread from heaven" the Son. The people died by what Moses gave and eternal life by what the Son gave. As it is written *"John 6:58*

"This is that bread which came down from heaven: not as your fathers did eat manna, and are dead: he that eateth of this bread shall live forever."
Moses said to hate thine enemy, "Yeshua says love thine enemy "Moses said there should be an" eye for an eye." *Yeshua says. Matt 5*

38 ¶Ye have heard that it hath been said, an eye for an eye, and a tooth for a tooth:
39 But I say unto you, that ye resist not evil: but whosoever shall smite thee on thy right cheek, turn to him the other also". Obviously there are differences here, but the point is that what Moses gave they only understood as to natural life, this is what is meant when the Word says teaching for doctrines the commandments of men.
For as it is written"

1 Then came to Jesus scribes and Pharisees, which were of Jerusalem, saying,

2 Why do thy disciples transgress the tradition of the elders? For they wash not their hands when they eat bread.

3 But he answered and said unto them, why do ye also transgress the commandment of God by your tradition?

4 For God commanded, saying, Honor thy father and mother: and, He that curseth father or mother, let him die the death.

5 But ye say, whosoever shall say to his father or his mother, It is a gift, by whatsoever thou mightest be profited by me;

6 And honour not his father or his mother, he shall be free. Thus have ye made the commandment of God of none effect by your tradition.

7 Ye hypocrites, well did Isaiah prophesy of you, saying,

8 This people draweth nigh unto me with their mouth, and honoureth me with their lips; but their heart is far from me.

9 But in vain they do worship me, teaching for doctrines the commandments of men".

Remember Yeshua was charged with sedition and heresy. So the Jews felt that he was changing their laws. For he also says:

21 ¶Ye have heard that it was said by them of old time, Thou shalt not kill; and whosoever shall kill shall be in danger of the judgment:

*22 But I say unto you, that whosoever is angry
with his brother without a cause shall be in danger
of the judgment:*
*"27 Ye have heard that it was said by them of old
time, Thou shalt not commit adultery:*
*28 But I say unto you, that whosoever looketh on a
woman to lust after her hath committed adultery
with her already in his heart.*

Moses law treated of the body, but Yeshua treats of the soul and body. Israel was not punished by what they thought or felt, but by what they spoke or did literally. So the Law of Moses was the same as Yeshua on a spiritual level, but different on a natural level. An eye for an eye spiritually meant to destroy anothers intellectual understanding from one's own affections of the evils of life. But naturally before the time Yeshua came it only referred to the physical eyes (That is the whole Law referred to a quality of life as to the body alone.) for they were not willing to nor could they understand spiritual things at that time being that they wanted to worship idol gods such as a golden calf, Baal, Molech, and others. For their minds did not pertain to heavenly life, but an earthly one only and a promise related to gold and silver. Otherwise they would not have followed Moses. Therefore the Law was given to them only in a natural sense while all along it held within it a spiritual sense which was revealed when Yeshua came, as it is written"

17¶Think not that I am come to destroy the law, or the prophets: I am not come to destroy, but to fulfill.
18 For verily I say unto you, Till heaven and earth pass, one jot or one tittle shall in no wise pass from the law, till all be fulfilled.
19 Whosoever therefore shall break one of these least commandments, and shall teach men so, he shall be called the least in the kingdom of heaven: but whosoever shall do and teach them, the same shall be called great in the kingdom of heaven.
20 For I say unto you, that except your righteousness shall exceed the righteousness of the scribes and Pharisees, ye shall in no case enter into the kingdom of heaven.

For their righteousness pertained to the body only and not to the soul (that is to the quality of the affections of life which one possesses for others as well as himself)

This is why an eye for an eye was given, because it corresponded to Divine order, which is that the hatred (evil affections) by which we destroy others the same is what destroys ourselves, for an evil affection or heart is the destruction of good therein and falsities of the understanding is the destruction of truth therein. Spiritual judgment is nothing else. This is why it is written *John 12:48*

He that rejecteth me, and receiveth not my words, hath one that judgeth him: the word that I have spoken, the same shall judge him in the last day.

"Matt 12:7 Therefore all things whatsoever ye would that men should do to you, do ye even so to them: for this is the law and the prophets.

28

The book of Revelation and things seen in the Spirit

To James: I do see your point. You are speaking concerning the miracles said to be done by the beast in Rev 13: and the prophecies that are in it. Although we know Satan does and can do actual miracles too. I do believe that Rev 13 is about something else that the term miracles and other things there written are referring to. I say this, because John the Apostle saw this in the Spirit, just as Ezekiel saw the dry bones in the Spirit. So they actually witnessed seeing and feeling what was happening as to their Spirit (for even there the angels spoke with him as also with Daniel). And as I know there is a real spiritual world, because Elijah asked the Lord to open Elisha's eyes to see the chariots of fire all around them by which they were protected, so John and Daniel and others eyes were opened to see the spiritual state of those at that time and of those to come. Paul himself had this experience when he said: In *1 cor 12:*

1 It is not expedient for me doubtless to glory. I will come to visions and revelations of the Lord.
2 I knew a man in Christ above fourteen years ago, (whether e in the body, I cannot tell; or whether out of the body, I cannot tell: God knoweth;) such an one caught up to the third heaven.
3 And I knew such a man, (whether in the body, or out of the body, I cannot tell: God knoweth;)
4 How that he was caught up into paradise, and heard unspeakable words, which it is not lawful for a man to utter.

Although they are visions, they are experienced as to the state of the mind/spirit and not of the body whereby, they could behold things in heaven and even in the earth things that are not visible to the natural eyes. The same thing happens when anyone sees an angel. They see them not with their physical eyes, but with their spiritual eye's opened. Consequently we could see them if our eyes were opened to see them.

My friend I do believe that the book of Daniel and Rev are describing the Doctrine of Devils and their power of persuasion to make what is false to appear true. For the purpose of miracles is to convince others of the validity of what they teach and that all this took place after the 3rd century when the Lord and the teachings of the Apostles were forsaken. So what I am saying is that wars described in the these books are not pointing to what is literal, but spiritual wars and battles as to what is true or false and as to what is good or evil. As we know the good and true win in the end which is described through the return of Yeshua. Consequently, I believe everything that was seen by them in the Spirit is in regard to nothing else, but what corresponds to spiritual things, which are doctrines and the love of them whether they be false or true. However, true doctrine and its teachings come from the Lord alone, for He is called the Word, which simply means that all spiritual good and truth come from him as its source. Consequently, the literal words of the bible correspond to spiritual truth and good which is from the Lord alone. Spiritual things are of the Spirit and the Lord is that Spirit from whom they proceed. The Spirit within the Lord is called the Divine and the Spirit that proceeds from him is called the Holy Spirit. There are not two Spirits just two different states of the Spirit. That which is the very Lord Himself which is called the Divine itself cannot be touched by man, for this is infinite, almighty and uncreated it is the Lord as He is in himself, this superior spiritual substance is called the Divine itself. That which proceeds from him is accommodated to the adaption of man whereby He is able to be among his creation and this is called the Spirit of God. The Lord alone as He is in himself is uncreated, but everything outside himself is created and brought into being. Anyone can see that that which is created is outside of that which is uncreated, for that which is uncreated was always there of itself. This state of the Spirit is greater and as was said before is called the Divine itself and is the Lord alone. However, that which proceeds from the Lord is not for himself, but for the sake of his creation that they may have life among themselves by him, whereby the state of the Spirit as to the created universe is called the Spirit of God. However, when the Lord suffered Himself to be born in the world it was then to be called the Holy Spirit. Therefore, the Lord is spiritually above all and all those who are of Him are born of the Spirit and they who are born of the Spirit are born of spiritual truth and love. These are the spiritual things and their qualities that are being referred to when the Word describes things that are said to be seen while one is said to be in the spirit.

29

More concerning the book of Revelation

To James: Yea I hear you. I do agree that it is also about what has and what is about to happen here on earth, but I just think it's referring to the doctrines that affect the whole world. Just think about it the Roman-catholic at one time ruled the world through the Pope even Kingdoms bowed down to her (except I believe France to a degree) until there was a breaking away from them by the reformed churches, but yet and still they took much of their doctrines with them except they no longer accepted the Pope as THE VICAR of Christ in the church. The beast as I see it refers spiritually to the evil and falsities of doctrine which men follow as to heart and mind. So does that mean the teachings of the Rom-catholic church? Or even of the reformed churches? And how they have deceived the whole Christendom that God is three and not one, that all are simply forgiven, because Yeshua died for all? And the whole world goes free? That faith alone saves without charity and good works at the same time saving? That no one can cooperate with the Lord as to choosing to obey Him concerning their salvation, but that this is a spiritual work that He does alone? I say Christendom, because the Word who alone is the Lord is also the Head of the church, and that this church is his Kingdom on earth. So, because this is the age or dispensation of Christ or of the Christian era it is referring to the atrocious doctrines that it has received. As it is written: *Rev 13:*

1 And I stood upon the sand of the sea, and saw a beast rise up out of the sea, having seven heads and ten horns, and upon his horns ten crowns, and upon his heads the name of blasphemy.

2 And the beast which I saw was like unto a leopard, and his feet were as the feet of a bear, and his mouth as the mouth of a lion: and the

dragon gave him his power, and his seat, and great authority.
And this over all Christendom wherever the Gospel was established which was mostly in Europe.

The animals of the bible

Notes*: It shouldn't be a wonder that the Word uses beasts or animals to represent spiritual affections. As for example the Lord likens his people to sheep and those who are not his people to wolves. That the children of Israel could only sacrifice and eat certain animals that were referred to as clean beasts and the others referred to as unclean beasts they were not to touch. As also with Noah some beasts were referred to as clean and others unclean. Also it speaks of the Lord making a covenant with the beasts of the field, in Hosea 2:18 it reads*
"And in that day will I make a covenant for them with the beasts of the field, and with the fowls of heaven, and with the creeping things of the ground: and I will break the bow and the sword and the battle out of the earth, and will make them to lie down safely."
Who cannot see that beasts have no rationality by which a covenant with them can be made? Or the beast with seven heads and ten horns in revelation. Or the Locust mentioned there with hair of women and the face of men and the teeth of lions. It should

be clear that the Word uses beasts in a representative way to described what is spiritually good and what is spiritually evil. This is why the Lord says in John 10:21 "My sheep hear my voice, and I know them and they follow me" it is clear that sheep are not meant, but that the Word uses the word sheep to signify those who are in good. Also in John 10:12

"12 But he that is an hireling, and not the shepherd, whose own the sheep are not, seeth the wolf coming, and leaveth the sheep, and fleeth: and the wolf catcheth them, and scattereth the sheep."

Anyone with sound reasoning can see that again actual sheep and wolves are not meant, but that this is an analogy, where the evil are likened to wolves and the good to sheep and that throughout the scriptures all animals are used to correspond to what is spiritually good or evil, depending on the nature of the beast that is used. Even where actual beasts are meant, they still correspond to spiritual good or evil, for the Word is holy on account of the spiritual concepts of which the natural historical events and words of the scriptures correspond to. And because the Word is holy it can never treat of natural things without spiritual concepts and ideas within it, for the Word is God and God is spirit (spiritual) and the spirit (spiritual) of God is holy and this is why the Word is holy and is referred to as the Holy Bible.

30

The Divine humanity of God

To Brian: I beg to differ, for before the incarnation there was only the Divine itself (YHWH) which no one could relate to except by types and figures such as the rituals that the Israelites had, also other nations had like rituals too in order to do this. Even Adam, for him being told not to eat of the tree of the knowledge of good and evil was a type or figure that related to him keeping a relationship with the Divine itself (YHWH). For what does natural food from a tree have to do with ones spiritual state? Except it be representative of one's spiritual state. What is for the body is for the body and what is for the soul is for the soul, as Paul say's "meat for the belly and belly for the meat, but God shall destroy them both." So now we see the Divine itself, (YHWH) standing alone apart from human emotions and feelings which came about with man by Him giving them a soul along with a corporal body which makes us human. The angels are hardly even considered to be human and how could the infinite Divine itself be. But after His incarnation as the scriptures tell us
Psalms 8:5

5 For thou hast made him a little lower than the angels, and hast crowned him with glory and honor and again,
Heb 2:9
9 But we see Jesus, who was made a little lower than the angels for the suffering of death, crowned with glory and honor; that he by the grace of God should taste death for every man.

How could He taste death for everyman unless by His spirit He was with everyman by which He could die for everyman? So the only way for YHWH to experience human emotion was to put on a human being by nature, by which he could experience sorrow and sadness like another man, compassion and anger like another man, but yet by His Divine/Spirit in the body, He controlled it all in a Divine way by which He overcame all and is crowned with glory and honor above all. Consequently, the Divine itself brought forth the Divine Human and this brought forth the Divine Proceeding which is called the Holy Spirit. These three make one Divine essence, which is God. The Divine itself called the Father. The Divine human called the Son and the Divine proceeding called the Holy Spirit.

Mans original life with God

Notes: Unless God (the Lord) had became human, no human would have been able to spiritually relate to him and thereby acknowledge him spiritually, for man had fallen from that spiritual place where He was able to recognize and receive God in a spiritual way without the need of God having to become born a man known as the Lord Jesus Christ. At that time they were without the need of alters and of animal sacrifices to worship God (such as the Israelites did, for they in fact were not a spiritual people, so by Divine providence God gave them the Law, which was full of spiritual representations whereby He might dwell among them until representations would be put away and the true spiritual would be given to men by the birth of Christ the Messiah), neither had they need of teachers and preachers or prophets, for the Lord dwelt with them (in their hearts and minds) in a special way so that they could be able to know and identify all things in creation, for at that time all of creation was in correspondence to spiritual good and truth, which is from the Lord alone. This is why Adam was able to identify every animal in the garden and give each one a name significant to their very nature and this without being taught by any man (Gen 2:19). This is why it also says that the female God gave him he identified her and called her women (Gen 2:23), because she was taken out of man, and that later he named her Eve which meant the mother of all living (Gen 3:20). Also, without being taught by any man, he already knew the concepts of marriage by saying in Gen 2:24 "Therefore shall a man leave his father and his mother, and shall cleave unto his wife: and they shall be one flesh."

Anyone can see that mankind had a unique relationship with God for mankind was created exactly as God had wanted them to be, which was in his image after his likeness. However, when man fell from this image, they could no longer relate to God in the wonderful manner in which they were created to. So they began to build alters of which nonetheless God gave them knowledge of by which they could identify and keep in mind a life of worship unto God. This began in the second generation of Adam with Cain and Able, but as their quality of life diminished so did the perception and knowledge they were receiving from God diminish until they had none and/or what they did have was corrupted and perverted in its use. At which time they were in need of a preacher who God called and sent by the name of Noah, however none were saved except those of his family.

31

What the torah taught compared to what Christ taught

To James: Also I must add that an eye for an eye is hardly the same as turning the other cheek to him that smites thee on the right cheek, The Torah taught to " *hate their enemies"* Christ taught to *"love your enemies"* completely opposite. However that is why the Torah was called the Law, for this retribution was after the flesh (for all those under the law are under the flesh, that is to live after the law (Torah) which was for the flesh), but turning the other cheek (which is nowhere mentioned in the Torah) emphasizes forgiveness and mercy, which is done not by the law, but by the Spirit of Christ. As it is written:

Jn 6: "Moses gave you not that bread from heaven; but my Father giveth you the true bread from heaven."

That the Torah did not treat of heavenly things, but earthly things. It did not treat of spiritual things, but natural things. It was not eternal, but temporal, waiting for the Spirit of Christ to take over.

But now we see that manna from heaven as it is written:

Jn 6:

35 And Jesus said unto them, I am the bread of life: he that cometh to me shall never hunger; and he that believeth on me shall never thirst.

So the Torah could not give Spiritual life (of which is meant never to hunger or thirst) only the Spirit of YHWH is able to give man a spiritual life. And the Spirit of Christ is that Spirit by which man has access to spiritual life which alone is from YHWH. And because this was different than what Moses taught. Yeshua therefore says *"New commandment I give unto you that ye love one another as I loved you"* For the whole Torah was about the laws of retribution a cheek for cheek, eye for eye, tooth for tooth, animal for animal and so on, so that the two are not the same at all for the law of retribution is not about forgiveness, but about the punishment of evil and the reward of their wicked ways. And their wicked ways was about hatred and not love, revenge and not forgiveness. Therefore Christ had to come and teach the doctrine of forgiveness and no more law of retribution (which really showed what they were about at heart) as they had done, but now as Yeshua says:

Matt 5

44 But I say unto you, Love your enemies, bless them that curse you, do good to them that hate you, and pray for them which despitefully use you, and persecute you;

45 That ye may be the children of your Father which is in heaven: for he maketh his sun to rise

*on the evil and on the good, and sendeth rain on
the just and on the unjust.
46 For if ye love them which love you, what
reward have ye? do not even the publicans the
same?
This is what Yeshua meant when He said:
John 13:34
34 A new commandment I give unto you, that ye
love one another; as I have loved you, that ye also
love one another.
John 15:12
12 This is my commandment, that ye love one
another, as I have loved you.*

32

No salvation in the Torah apart from Christ

To James: *Roman 7:*
*4 "Wherefore, my brethren, ye also are become
dead to the law by the body of Christ; that ye
should be married to another, even to him who is
raised from the dead, that we should bring forth
fruit unto God.
5 For when we were in the flesh, the motions of
sins, which were by the law, did work in our
members to bring forth fruit unto death*

6 But now we are delivered from the law, that being dead wherein we were held; that we should serve in newness of spirit and not in the oldness of the letter ".

For one it is false to teach that without the shedding of blood there is remission of sins. This is against the Torah and the Prophets throughout. For as it is written:

Lev 17:

11 For the life of the flesh is in the blood: and I have given it to you upon the altar to make an atonement for your souls: for it is the blood that maketh an atonement for the soul.

Hebrews 9:22

22 And almost all things are by the law purged with blood; and without shedding of blood is no remission of sins.

Second, What? The Torah existed before the foundation of the world? I know you would like to believe that but that is totally made up and against scripture. The Torah is the history and the law and prophets that were given to Israel which could not come into existence until after creation. Do you not know the gentiles as well as the Hebrews knew about animal sacrifices and also had laws and commandments of like rituals? Do you really think the Ten Commandments came into existence through Moses? And that those other nations did not already have those same laws? Abraham and his whole family worshiped different gods anyway. Thereafter he was called by YHWH. Now all knowledge of everything was with YHWH before creation, but the Spirit of YHWH was actually before the foundation of the world and this Spirit is the Spirit of Christ which existed before creation for as it was written:

John 17:24

24 Father, I will that they also, whom thou hast given me, be with me where I am; that they may behold my glory, which thou hast given me: for thou lovedst me before the foundation of the world.

Jn 17:

5 And now, O Father, glorify thou me with thine own self with the glory which I had with thee before the world was.

Even those under the Torah at that time looked to the salvation of Yeshua for without him or without looking to Him there is no salvation. Not for them in the OT nor for them in the NT, for the Torah was for the body, but the Spirit of Christ is for the soul and body, apart from such, there is no salvation, for the soul is the true essence of a person's life. This is true especially for the Jew, for if He denies the one and only Soul Savior. How can they be saved? Consequently they are utterly lost and are yet wandering in the wilderness and shall die in their sins, because they refuse to acknowledge the Soul Savior, as He says:

John 8:24

24 I said therefore unto you, that ye shall die in your sins: for if ye believe not that I am he, ye shall die in your sins.

So apart from Yeshua the Torah cannot save you, for he is the Alpha and Omega, the beginning and the end, not the Torah.

33

Dead to the Law!

To John: You have a false explanation of this chapter my friend. It did not say Israel died to the Law by being an adulterous nation. He instead is showing that there were two scenarios to the outcome of coming out from under the law. One was by being labeled and adulterer and therefore judged to death and condemnation, or the other was by the death of the husband, by which there would be no judgment, but the wife would be free from the law and would be able to marry again, in fact to a much better husband than the law.

Rom 7:2, 3

2 For the woman which hath an husband is bound by the law to her husband so long as he liveth; but if the husband be dead, she is loosed from the law of her husband.

3 So then if, while her husband liveth, she be married to another man, she shall be called an adulterous: but if her husband be dead, she is free from that law; so that she is no adulteress, though she be married to another man".

You must understand that Christ was born under the Law and He also died by that same Law. So it is not Israel that died, but the body of Christ that died not just for him, but for all who were under the law. Whereby, Israel is dead to the Law, by the body of Christ that died, and this for himself and for all under the law. Wherefore we are married to the resurrected Savior who rose from the dead free from the law. Therefore Christ death was the death of those who are under the law and his resurrection is our new marriage to the risen Christ who is freed from the law by his own death, whereby making us free from the law, for our death is in him to the law, but our new marriage is in him unto the newness of the Spirit, made possible by his resurrected new body. Therefore the law was limited, because it could not supply the power to live by it or bring forth fruit unto YHWH.

Rom 7:3,4

4 Wherefore, my brethren, ye also are become dead to the law by the body of Christ; that ye should be married to another, even to him who is raised from the dead, that we should bring forth fruit unto God.

5 For when we were in the flesh, the motions of sins, which were by the law, did work in our members to bring forth fruit unto death.

6 But now we are delivered from the law, that being dead wherein we were held; that we should serve in newness of spirit, and not in the oldness of the letter.

34

The Law of Moses replaced by the grace and truth of Christ

To John: you need to go over that more slowly. You are absolutely misunderstanding this whole chapter. It is saying that they died to the law through the death of Christ who came under the law and died as to it. So that there is a new husband we are married to now. This is why he says

Rom 7:2,4

2 For the woman which hath an husband is bound by the law to her husband so long as he liveth; but if the husband be dead, she is loosed from the law of her husband.

and goes on to say

4 Wherefore, my brethren, ye also are become dead to the law by the body of Christ; that ye should be married to another, even to him who is raised from the dead, that we should bring forth fruit unto God.

Everyone knows Israel was an adulterous nation. That is why the prophet was told to marry a harlot who repeatedly committed adultery on him, but the prophet was ordered to take her back and not have her killed. Had Israel died for adultery (that is as an adulterous nation) none of them would have been around today. So they had to die to the law to free them from death that was brought on by the law. The death that was brought on by the law is nothing else other than that it was manifested in their lives that they could not keep the law due to it being weak through the flesh for sin is from the will of one's spirit in the flesh and not from the flesh itself. So in order to keep them from living this way continuously, that is, in death which was the life the prophet's wife had, Yeshua had to replace the law and the prophets by the death of the Old Testament (Old man being body of Christ) which was born under the law, and replace it by the New Testament, which is the new man who was resurrected without the law, having a new body which was made Divine (spiritual) unlike the old body which came under the law and was made earthly trying to obey heavenly laws with an earthly mind, which they could never do for the Torah signified things that pertained to heavenly/spiritual things in an earthly way and because they were not heavenly/spiritual they could not maintain it in an earthly way. Yeshua who came with an heavenly/spiritual quality from above was able to maintain it in an earthly way and was able to fulfill the law by dying without sin, whereby a new dispensation began in him who fulfilled all things and became the head of all righteousness and holiness and thus He imparts this heavenly/spiritual quality of life, which is from above to all who looked to him for it. So that it is not the Torah anymore that condemns a man or justifies him, but Christ that died. *Rom 8: 34Who is he that condemneth? It is Christ that died, yea rather, that is risen again, who is even at the right hand of God, who also maketh intercession for us.*

That which is said to be dead just means it has moved on and evolved into the new and that which is said to be new is not necessarily new it's just brought forth in a new way.

35

Miracles

To James: Although as you mentioned Satan does perform false miracles. My idea of a false miracle is one not Divine. Outwardly they appear the same in every aspect such as what it says in *Matt 7: 22 Many will say to me in that day, Lord, Lord, have we not prophesied in thy name? and in thy name have cast out devils? And in thy name done many wonderful works?*
23 And then will I profess unto them, I never knew you: depart from me, ye that work iniquity.
Consequently signs and wonders were used to confirm truth as it says in *Mk 16:*

*20 " And they went forth, and preached
everywhere, the Lord working with them, and
confirming the word with signs following. Amen. "*
Therefore Satan does these same miracles to
confirm what is false as it says in *Rev 13:*
*13 And he doeth great wonders, so that he maketh
fire come down from heaven on the earth in the
sight of men,*
*14 And deceiveth them that dwell on the earth by
the means of those miracles which he had power to
do in the sight of the beast; saying to them that
dwell on the earth, that they should make an image
to the beast, which had the wound by a sword, and
did live.*

Not to mention Egypt's magicians doing some
of the same miracles as Moses himself did.
Yes they appeared the same, but the difference as
we know was that Egypt looked to their gods and
Moses looked to YHWH. So therefore, I would
conclude that as we are looking to the Lord in
worship and fellowship in the Spirit, as we are
delighting ourselves in him, Satan cannot abide
with the person who does this from a pure heart.
Consequently, the Lords presence is increased with
the person and He therefore begins to operate
through that person unto the good of all. Therefore,
where the Spirit of the Lord abides, Satan cannot
have his way. For the Spirit (which is from above
and from the Divine) is Joy Peace and happiness in

the Lord and where these are present, Satan cannot have his way. As Yeshua says in *Luke 11:*
18 If Satan also be divided against himself, how shall his kingdom stand? Because ye say that I cast out devils through Beelzebub.
19And if I by Beelzebub cast out devils, by whom do your sons cast them out? Therefore, shall they be your judges.
20 But if I with the finger of God cast out devils, no doubt the kingdom of God is come upon you.

Blessed are all they whose delight is in the Lord day and night for He fills them with Divine Joy, peace and Happiness whereby Satan cannot function or operate through them, for the fountain is either fresh water or salt, but it cannot be both at the same time. Let us remain fresh so the Lord can continue to use us without interference from Satan.

36

The express image of his person

Hebrews 1:3
3" Who being the brightness of his glory, and the express image of his person, and upholding all things by the word of his power, when he had by himself purged our sins, sat down on the right hand of the Majesty on high;"

To James: The Divine is omnipresent. It is in all space apart from space, in all time apart from time. Space came forth from the infinity and time from eternity. Therefore space and time and all things in creation are images of some aspect of the Divine, because they were all brought forth by him alone. The Divine is infinite, uncreated from eternity to eternity. The Divine is uncreated, but man and angel are created. Therefore the Divine is infinite, but man and angel finite. There is no ratio between the finite and infinite. Consequently there is no comparison, except in an image or likeness or analogy or correspondence, and yet after all that, in the end they are still, only images (representations) and not the real thing nor ever can be. The Spirit or Soul is the real thing of a person's life. The body is only an outward image of that life which it uses for transactions in this world. The body is the image of one's soul. However, the phrase "express image of his person" is just that or "The brightness of his glory". Who cannot see that when a puppet is being used by the puppet master the expressions of the puppet are not its own? The personality, Characteristics, even all things of the nature of the Master is being expressed in the puppet. If the Puppet Master has all Power, Wisdom and Glory in heaven and in earth, then the puppet will come into the same things. All the other puppets are expressions of their own souls. Everyone's body is a puppet possessed by its own soul, which is its puppet master. This is why he says: *Matt 23:* *"8 But be not ye called Rabbi: for one is you're Master, even Christ; and all ye are brethren.*

9 And call no man your father upon the earth: for one is your Father, which is in heaven.
10 Neither be ye called masters: for one is your Master, even Christ."
This is, because Christ is the Spiritual man controlling the natural man.

Because His body (the image) was produced or brought forth it was called The Son. While the Life of that body was called the Father and because it was his Son that was being used to communicate with man it was said in *John 14*
7 If ye had known me, ye should have known my Father also: and from henceforth ye know him, and have seen him.
8 Philip saith unto him, Lord, shew us the Father, and it sufficeth us.
9 Jesus saith unto him, have I been so long time with you, and yet hast thou not known me, Philip? he that hath seen me hath seen the Father; and how sayest thou then, Shew us the Father?
10 Believest thou not that I am in the Father, and the Father in me? The words that I speak unto you I speak not of myself: but the Father that dwelleth in me, he doeth the works. Also it was said:
Matthew 11:27
All things are delivered unto me of my Father: and no man knoweth the Son, but the Father; neither knoweth any man the Father, save the Son, and he to whomsoever the Son will reveal him.

How could this be if he was just another man? For men know men just as they knew Moses and the Prophets and all the Kings, why can't man know him unless He reveals himself to man? This is what it is to be the Express image of his person" this is why He is called by the prophet Isaiah *"The Everlasting Father"*. As for being *"the brightness of His glory"* it is written"
Revelation 21:23
And the city had no need of the sun, neither of the moon, to shine in it: for the glory of God did lighten it and the Lamb is the light thereof.

37

The way to understand Old Testament Scriptures!

(It was strongly explained by someone that the God of the Old Testament was very unloving, unkind and cruel)

To Brian: It is your teaching my brother that makes YHWH out to be evil and wicked, and even cruel. It is you and those who think like you that take the bible in a literal way and cannot see beyond the vial that was torn down when Yeshua our Lord and Savior came. Just as the Jews of Yeshua time would have killed him for making himself equal to YHWH, for it is written in John 10:22-31 22

" *And it was at Jerusalem the feast of the dedication, and it was winter.*

23 And Jesus walked in the temple in Solomon's poch.

24 Then came the Jews round about him, and said unto him, how long dost thou make us to doubt? If thou be the Christ, tell us plainly.

25 Jesus answered them, I told you, and ye believed not: the works that I do in my Father's name, they bear witness of me.

26 But ye believe not, because ye are not of my sheep, as I said unto you.

27 My sheep hear my voice, and I know them, and they follow me:

28 And I give unto them eternal life; and they shall never perish; neither shall any man pluck them out of my hand.

29 My Father, which gave them me, is greater than all; and no man is able to pluck them out of my Father's hand.

30 I and my Father are one.

31 Then the Jews took up stones again to stone him

32 Jesus answered them, Many good works have I shewed you from my Father; for which of those works do ye stone me?

33 The Jews answered him, saying, for a good work we stone thee not; but for blasphemy; and because that thou, being a man, makest thyself God. "

You are stuck and cannot be enlightened in any further. Then also it is you who believes exactly what it says word for word without any Spirit of truth from Yeshua guiding us as was taught by Yeshua himself that the Spirit of truth receives from Him and gives it to us. All of the word is YHWH and needs to be taught by Yeshua or else all will believe as you do that it is YHWH who kills and is unmerciful and is cruel to all that do not obey him, which is no different than any other common dictator. For in 1 *Samuel 15: 2-3* it reads:

2 Thus saith the Lord of hosts, I remember that which Amalek did to Israel, how he laid wait for him in the way, when he came up from Egypt. 3Now go and smite Amalek, and utterly destroy all that they have, and spare them not; but slay both man and woman, infant and suckling, ox and sheep, camel and ass.

Why murder and kill infants who know not whither they come or Go? Or the sons of Aaron who were destroyed and consumed by fire from YHWH (as it is written) simply because they got fire from a different place other than the alter. Surely you don't believe the fire they were supposed to get was holy of itself. Or could it be that it represented doing all things from the holiness of love found in Yeshua and unto all those that would believe in him and do his commandments, for as it was written he came to fulfill the law and the prophets for he is the fullness of the law and the prophet's. What you should take literally is what Daniel wrote, Dan.7:13-14, 27 say's" *I saw and behold one like the son of man came with clouds of heaven, and there was given him dominion, and glory, and a kingdom, that ALL PEOPLES AND NATIONS, AND LANGUAGES MAY WORSHIP HIM:* Or does that not include you too? How can you put a blind eye to this, when it is in front of your face? Beware lest there be found hypocrisy in you. For all without the guidance of Yeshua's spirit make YHWH out to be EVIL and WICKED. Especially the Israelites who at that time refused to obey simple instruction. For it was not YHWH who was wicked, but the mindset of them and those like them that was wicked and evil, for they could not receive the Law in any other way. Being all together natural corporeal thinkers they could not understand YHWH in any other way. So YHWH was with them only in the way that they could receive Him. The whole Law was given to them only in the way they could receive it, for they were idolaters and adulterous in nature. That is why Yeshua said to them, *"because of the hardness of your heart Moses gave you the precept for divorce, but in the beginning it was not so. "* But because of the hardness their heart and those who think like them the whole Law was given like it was given and YHWH did and said what he did among them the way that He did, because this was their mindset and not God's, and also due to the fact that a representative church was instituted among them. Therefore, because of this He permitted these things to be for the sake of the preservation of the human race until the fullness of times (thus a new dispensation) should come when Yeshua would come and do away with those Laws and the OT ways and bring in Grace and Truth Divine whereby we are cleansed not by the blood of bulls and lambs, but by the life, death and resurrection of YESHUA YHWH among us.

38

There is only one true and living God

To Mark: My friend Apostle Paul more than others explains that Yeshua is YHWH who has come. Most of his epistles more than others explain this. It is all throughout Colossians, Hebrews, Corinthians, Thessalonians, and more, but to the point,

Acts 14:15

That ye should turn from these vanities unto the LIVING GOD, which made heaven and earth and the sea and all things that are there in.

It was common for Iconium to regard especially strangers as gods among the Greeks and later in Rome. There were beliefs in their myths that the gods would come among them disguised as mortals. Paul simply wanted them to turn away from those vanities of the mythology and turn to something real and pure. However for him to take the time to explain this, well there was no time. For by the time he persuaded them not to sacrifice unto him. The Jews in that area and also from Antioch turned the people against him to stone him. Things that are not said do not mean that they are not true. Neither does it mean that things are not true when we think they should have been said.

John 16:12- Yeshua say's "I have yet many things to say unto you, but ye cannot bear them now.
13 Howbeit when he, the spirit of truth, is come, he will guide you into all truth: for he shall not speak of himself; but whatsoever he shall hear, that shall he speak: and he will shew you things to come.
14He shall glorify me: for he shall receive of mine, and shall shew it unto you.
15All things that the Father hath are mine: therefore said I, that he shall take of mine, and shall shew it unto you.
16 A little while, and ye shall not see me: and again, a little while, and ye shall see me, because I go to the Father.

How can the Spirit of truth receive guidance from Yeshua if Yeshua is not YHWH? Who cannot see this? What things does the Father have that is Yeshua's also? What is the Spirit of truth taking from Yeshua and showing to us? Who is telling the Spirit of truth what to say? Perhaps

Yeshua is the Divine Wisdom of YHWH and the Spirit of truth is the enlightenment that comes from that Divine wisdom. Furthermore, Father is The Divine Love of YHWH. So know we can see how that *"ALL THINGS THAT THE FATHER HATH ARE MINE: THEREFORE SAID I, THAT HE SHALL TAKE OF MINE AND SHOW IT UNTO YOU"* The literal sense of the Word corresponds to Divine attributes that belong to the Divine itself alone. For the Word is first Divine, then heavenly (spiritual), then natural or literal for the Word is YHWH made flesh and the Word is the Spirit of truth that enlightens all men. The literal Word is not the same as the spiritual, nor the spiritual the same as the Divine. These are different degrees of the same Word which all tie back to the Divine itself which is and who is the Word.

39

"In the Beginning was the Word and the Word was with God and the Word was God"

To Brian: The Word that is God is also with God. Because the Word is from Him it is with Him. That same Word became flesh and is known as *"Emmanuel God with us"*, also *"Prince of Peace, Everlasting Father"* who doesn't know these scriptures. *"When you see me you see the Father"*. *"No one has seen the father nor his shape, but the son who has revealed him"*. Reveal is to manifest in the flesh. The Father and the Son are one. Just as soul and body are one. Two states of life, but only one Life, therefore only one God. It was not until God was perfected as to the flesh that he said all power is given unto me in heaven and in earth. All men have a spiritual and natural body. Why not Almighty God? That is if man is created in his image. And so behold, He fulfilled that and came as a man to have also a spiritual and natural body. His spiritual body was the Divine spiritual itself and his natural body, being that it was produced was called the Son of the Living God. Therefore He was named Jesus and Christ *"For he will save his people from their sins"*. Remember as someone mentioned *"There is no savior besides me and my glory I will not give to another".* If this is true then Jesus Christ was with God and was God, and in time manifested himself in the flesh to all as God's Son. Consequently that which we see is called the Son and that which we cannot see is called the Father. *"Show us the father and it will suffice us He answered when you see me you see the Father".* Howbeit, this was not fulfilled until He was glorified or resurrected and became fully divine even as to His body, whereby he was then able to disappear and reappear at will, which meant that his Divine and His body became one and the same. This was noted especially when He ascended, because then He had put off everything earthly and had put on fully the Divine itself. This is what He meant when He said he was going back to the Father, also when He prayed to have the glory he once had with Father before the world was. Although, as to his body He is identified as the Son who is with the Father, yet and still He is called *"The everlasting Father".* So as the Word was God it was also with God and is always among men. As He said *"Lo I am with you always even unto the end of the world".*

40

An explanation of reincarnation as to a religion called Spiritism

(Spiritism is a religion that believes that most of us born into the world are souls that were here before, thus reincarnated and this continually until the individual comes into the state of life he was meant to have)

To Anna: I have indeed looked into Spritism' my dear and have some things to say concerning it. I believe I have grown much in my understanding since the last time we have seen each other. I can give better clarity as to the things I speak of more so now than before. Thereby, bringing more understanding to the things that I speak of, for those who do hear me, wither they, that is my words be true or false, for all things that are said to be true art to be compared against those things which are also said to be true in order to see rationally which is sound and which is not. However, Spiritism seems to be a compilation of many things together. I would like to point out that my understanding is that the spirit world and the natural world were created together. So in a like image of this, every soul and its own body are also procreated together. These souls take on inherited spiritual and natural qualities from their parents and these are developed as they grow and mature in age. The parents themselves (that is, the substances of their life, which are devoid of intrinsic life) from which or through which these souls proceed are for the first time being developed with these newly procreated bodies. The new bodies themselves are signatures of the new souls that inhabit them, both brought forth and developed together at birth. After death the soul is no longer new as it was in its beginning, therefore a new body by birth cannot be given it. Because the soul has developed beyond this stage it must continue its spiritual life in a spiritual body apart from a natural one. His body was only a vehicle to get him to his destination which is the Spiritual world, after that eternity there. When souls depart from their original encasing (body), because it is so unique it cannot be reincarnated through another. However, it can enter a living body and thereby speak to others by possession. Consequently, by the sharing of that body with whom it belongs to and this only temporally, because it is not his own. He his eventually cast out in one way or the other. All souls produce bodies that are images of themselves. Because souls are procreated through parents, they are progressions of the substances of the life of the parents, whereby the seed is a byproduct of the parents, which concludes that they are solely procreated from them alone and could not come from a spirit reincarnated from the world of spirits or from any place else for that matter. Spirits exists in the world of spirits the same as human beings exists on here on earth, the only difference is that the latter is temporal and former is eternal.

The progressions of the soul cannot change course once they leave the body, for man is created in the image of God, for as it is written
Malachi 3:6
6 For I am the Lord, I change not;
That is, as to life, God is divine love and divine wisdom and His life does not change. So man after the death of the body is also a spirit as God is a spirit and therefore like God into whose image we were created, man's life cannot change, but progresses more and more as to the same quality of life he had when he was in the world. So long as the spirit of man is dwelling in the body he can change his quality of life, due to the fact that the spirit being in the body is not yet in an eternal state as to its quality of life. This is because the body to which it is attached is not eternal, but temporal. Therefore the quality of the life of one's spirit is also temporal until they leave the body, at which point the state in which they have died stays with them throughout eternity. This is why it is said that if you die in sin without repentance, which is to have a change of heart, your soul will be lost forever. For natural laws are subject to spiritual laws and because they are of different laws, changes must be allowed to the natural in order for it to constantly meet the standards of the

spiritual. But spiritual laws are subject to Divine order which never changes and because spiritual laws are subjected to Divine order they too can never change, consequently the spiritual life of man after he has left his body (being spiritual) will never change, but remain subject to the same spiritual laws, which are subject to God who is a Spirit and who too never changes.

41
Purgatory

To Anna: Wow. I feel for you and I do understand what you are saying and I agree there are many teachings out there, but I believe that Pure Divine truth makes more sense to the mind than anything else out there, but how do we know that we have it? We must indeed go over these teachings with prayer so that our rationality is enlightened to see all things clearly.
I am glad you spoke to the catholic priest, because it helps to get an understanding of where they are coming from. As I thought, they claim God forgives you, but you do not escape punishment. This is not spiritual forgiveness. When you are forgiven a debt that you owe, you do not have to pay it back.
Matt 18:23-27

23¶Therefore is the kingdom of heaven likened unto a certain king, which would take account of his servants.

24And when he had begun to reckon, one was brought unto him, which owed him ten thousand talents.

25 But forasmuch as he had not to pay, his lord commanded him to be sold, and his wife, and children, and all that he had, and payment to be made.

26The servant therefore fell down, and worshipped him, saying, Lord, have patience with me, and I will pay thee all.

27Then the lord of that servant was moved with compassion, and loosed him, and forgave him the debt.

So according to this scripture, what the Catholic Church is teaching is false. To be forgiven of our sins is also to be loosed from the punishment of sin, for then we are truly forgiven. What the Catholic Church teaches is what is in the rest of that chapter which is

Matt 18:28-35

28But the same servant went out, and found one of his fellow servants, which owed him an hundred pence: and he laid hands on him, and took him by the throat, saying, Pay me that thou owest.

29And his fellow servant fell down at his feet, and besought him, saying, Have patience with me, and I will pay thee all.

30And he would not: but went and cast him into prison, till he should pay the debt.
31So when his fellow servants saw what was done, they were very sorry, and came and told unto their lord all that was done.
32Then his lord, after that he had called him, said unto him, O thou wicked servant. I forgave thee all that debt, because thou desirest me:
33 Shouldest not thou also have had compassion on thy fellow servant, even as I had pity on thee?
34And his lord was wroth, and delivered him to the tormentors, till he should pay all that was due unto him.
35 So likewise shall my heavenly Father do also unto you, if ye from your hearts forgive not everyone his brother their trespasses.

So see, our sufferings come from not having a likeness of the nature of God, for had he at heart received the spirit of forgiveness in his own life, he would have also given it to others who needed it. Therefore, he never genuinely received God's forgiveness and when judgment day came he was cast into hell until he paid up in full. However, after death whatever is in the inmost part of the heart can never come out so they will pay for all eternity, but there are others whose inmost part of the heart is in genuine forgiveness, but the outer parts are not the same so they undergo a process to fully become what their inmost heart is so that the outer parts of the heart are shed off leaving the inmost part to remain forever, for this is their true nature before they died. After which they enter heaven for ever. So really one is either saved when he dies or lost. There is no in between only a process to become what he really is at heart. This process is called judgment day, after which the evil is cast into hell and the good are raised into heaven.

42

Holiness inwardly is Holiness outwardly

To Melvin: It is understood that God cannot fail, because there is no failure in him. God says in the scriptures that He is holy so therefore there can be no unholiness in him. What a person is in his essence he also is as to his whole being. The Word is not holy, because of its literal sense, but because of its spiritual sense. This is because God is a spirit and since his spirit is holy the spiritual sense which comes from the spirit is also holy, and because the natural sense comes from this it is holy also. It is the heart or the essence of a man that makes the quality of a man and not the body of the man. Change the heart or the essence of the man then you change the man himself, never the other way around. What is holy in its inmost is also holy in

its outmost, not because of the outmost itself, but
because of the inmost from which it proceeds.
What is pure at heart or in essence cannot make
things impure, because this is against its nature.
Unholiness comes from being disconnected from
what is holy. The bible is holy or the Torah is holy
because it is connected to what is holy. Whenever
the Word came to the prophets, it would say that
the word of the Lord came to them and as we
know the essence of the Lord is holy, therefore his
Word which comes forth from him is also holy for
as he says *"the word that I speak unto you they are
spirit and they are life"*. His spirit is holy therefore
his word which is spirit is also holy. The Torah the
Bible and even people only become unholy,
because of being separated from God who alone is
holy. The letter killeth when it is separated from
the spirit which giveth life. All things are unholy
of themselves when they are separated from God.
But God cannot make anything unholy or impure
or unrighteous, because none of these exist in his
will or life or nature, for himself nor for others, but
men do this of themselves and not of the Lord. It is
understood that a tree is known by its fruit .The
essence of the tree is also in its fruit and this again
is in its seed which in turn becomes a tree again.
What is in the seed is also in the tree and this also
is in the fruit. Holiness inwardly also means
holiness outwardly for it is the inward man that
determines the quality of the outward man no

matter how it may appear on the outside. Also I should mention it is not man nor Angel that makes the Word holy, but the Spirit of God who inspires them. The words come from this and therefore the words are from holiness itself for they are from within Him, for as it is written: *"In the beginning was the Word and the Word was with God and the Word was God"*. God and his Word are the same. The Word which is from God is an extension of Himself from Himself out to others and even to all who will receive him.

43

God cannot create unholy things

To Melvin: The Lord say's in his Word
Malachi 3:6
For I am the Lord, I change not.
God is not like man. With God there is only what is and what is not. God says be ye holy for I am Holy. God wants all things and people to be as himself, Holy. Therefore, God would not make people or anything in creation unholy, for love wants to share all things it is and has with all others. How much more God, who is love itself. There is no power in God to fail, because there is no power in failure. So therefore there is no power in God to make man or anything for that matter unholy. People become unholy of themselves. That

which God declares unholy was always unholy, for
the principles of what is unholy are meant and
these are not from God, but from a life discordant
with God. If God created good and evil as you say,
which is indeed the question? So did he? Or did
God create man who on his own free will chooses
good or evil for himself, and thus create good or
evil for himself as to his own life, for thorns and
thistles came after Adam fell not before it, Cain
killed Seth after the fall of man and not before it.
Man can only do good and evil of himself in a
natural way, but never from himself in a spiritual
way, for spiritual good is holy, for all spiritual
good and truth is from and by the Holy Spirit.

44

Your sexual orientation and life

Obviously we are all born with distinguished characteristics. We are all born generally either male or female apart from some who are born with abnormalities due to some genetic dysfunction or birth defect. All are born from the intercourse of heterosexual experience. None are born apart from this. The sperm from the male and egg from the female must be from a heterosexual (heterogeneous) biological nature, in order for them to adjoin or connect together (this is what the term hetero means), by this the two become one and thus make one person. A part from heterosexual biological interaction the sperm being part of the male biological make up and the egg being part of the female biological make up, there can be no reproduction or procreation of any kind. Homogeneous being not of connecting parts, but of like parts cannot adjoin and therefore cannot reproduce anything. This is a scientific fact not an opinion. This is so even on a biological level such as the cellular structure and is true of all homogeneous interaction. Heterogeneous are like parts to a puzzle that fit together. Homogeneous parts are like building blocks that are of the same structure so instead of fitting together like pieces of a puzzle they add to each other by making layers vertically or horizontally. An example of this would be how the bodies muscles are made up of fibers and these are made up of fibrils. They are made of the same structure, but are just bundled in a way so as to make larger compiles to support the whole and in this case the larger compile is called muscle. Now just as it takes two European parents to make a European baby, it also takes a pair of heterosexual bodies to produce a baby with a heterosexual body. That pair would be male and female which are heterosexually compatible to each other, which in turn would produce something from itself which is heterosexual in order to continue reproducing. Therefore homosexuality is a state of the body, only because it is a state one's mind, nevertheless the body because it proceeds from heterosexual interaction is itself heterosexual.

No one is born knowing what they are, for the human brain at that point is not developed for thought process, but as this develops so they become who they believe they are to be, so although the body is clearly heterosexual in itself. It is not the body that thinks, but the mind in the body is what thinks. Consequently there are some who are born male, but later reason in their minds that they are female and undergo sex changes to bring their bodies into agreement with their minds. There are also those who believe in bestiality (that is they believe in having sex with animals), likewise homosexuality, although such interaction cannot reproduce anything. So although the human body is itself heterosexual, the mind can still reject this. The mind only consists of what it has learned and experienced. From this the beliefs of that mind forms the judgment of oneself and of others. We should subject our minds and our life to what God openly created us to be and not subject our bodies and our life to a mind that is contrary to this.